The U.S. Women's Soccer Team

The U.S. Women's Soccer Team

An American Success Story

Second Edition

Clemente A. Lisi

TAYLOR TRADE PUBLISHING
Lanham • New York • Boulder • Toronto • Plymouth, UK

Published by Taylor Trade Publishing
An imprint of The Rowman & Littlefield Publishing Group, Inc.
4501 Forbes Boulevard, Suite 200, Lanham, Maryland 20706
www.rowman.com

10 Thornbury Road, Plymouth PL6 7PP, United Kingdom

Distributed by National Book Network

British Library Cataloguing in Publication Information Available

Library of Congress Cataloging-in-Publication Data

Lisi, Clemente Angelo, 1975–
  The U.S. women's soccer team : an American success story / Clemente
A. Lisi. — 2nd ed.
    p. cm.
  Includes bibliographical references and index.
  ISBN 978-1-58979-711-6 (pbk. : alk. paper)
  1. U.S. Women's National Soccer Team—History. 2. Women soccer
players—United States—Biography. 3. Soccer for women—United States.
I. Title.
  GV944.5.L57 2013
  796.3340922—dc23
  [B]

2012040154

∞™ The paper used in this publication meets the minimum requirements
of American National Standard for Information Sciences—Permanence of
Paper for Printed Library Materials, ANSI/NISO Z39.48-1992.

Printed in the United States of America

To my son, Mark—you are such a gift

Contents

Foreword by *Danielle Fotopoulos*   vii

Acknowledgments   xi

Introduction   xiii

1   Top of the World   1

2   Norwegian Heartbreak   22

3   The Golden Girls   39

4   Party Like It's 1999   52

5   Feeling Down Under   72

6   Revenge   83

7   New World Order   95

8   Going Solo   108

9   Top of the World Again   120

10   Golden Again   130

Appendix A: U.S. Women's National Team Year-by-Year
All-Time Results, 1985–2012   151

Appendix B: U.S. Women's National Team All-Time Team
Leaders, 1985–2012   167

Index   169

About the Author   171

Foreword

Danielle Fotopoulos

For me, the dream of playing for the United States started when I was just thirteen and had to choose between basketball and soccer. I chose soccer. I knew that I made the right choice given that I had been fortunate enough to grow up next to Michelle Akers, one of the greatest female soccer players the United States has ever produced. I lived in Altamonte Springs, Florida, and she lived in nearby Oviedo at the time. I got to shag balls for her, and she let me attend Post-to-Post soccer camp. This is where, at age fourteen, I made friends with future U.S. teammates Marci Miller and Kate Sobrero. We stayed good friends throughout our time together on the team. Soccer can sometimes be such a small world. Most soccer people know one another or know of one another. It is a world that has been a huge part of my life but not the only part.

Fetching balls for Michelle Akers built character in me and made me see the hard work and dedication it took to be the best. She trained and trained. Repetition was the key for her and still is. Michelle was constantly working on her skills, touches, passes, and finishing. She was a master at finishing the ball. She was a specimen in the air. I can always remember looking up to her and wanting to be like her. I once stood in line in Baltimore, Maryland, for thirty minutes just to get her autograph. She knew me and we chatted for a bit. She was a big motivator and became my role model. Eventually, she went from being my role model to a teammate. I was competing alongside her on the same team. I could only think one thing: *Awesome!*

I got the call to join the national team when I was just a college sophomore at Southern Methodist University. I can remember getting the message that U.S. coach Tony DiCicco had called and wanted to invite me—*me!*—into the next training camp in Chula Vista, California. I was so excited when I got the message that I called him back right away to let him know that I accepted his invite. However, I forgot that there was a one-hour time difference separating him in Boston from me in Texas. I woke him up at 10:00 PM.

I was so excited that I blurted out, "I accept your offer to come into camp and thank you for the opportunity."

"You're welcome. Can we talk about this tomorrow?" he replied.

I said, "Sure. And sorry I woke you. Thanks again!"

That is how my exciting—and unforgettable journey—began. My first training camp, in January 1995, was awesome. I was so nervous and excited, all at the same time. At first, I had no idea what to expect. "Do my best!" was all I could think—the advice my dad gave me. I also thought, "Have fun!"—the advice my mom gave me.

When I got to camp, I was expecting to see Akers, Mia Hamm, Julie Foudy, Kristine Lilly, Joy Fawcett, and Carla Overbeck. I was both relieved and disappointed that they were not in. Instead, I was there with Christie Pearce, Lori Fair, Saskia Webber, Tiffeny Roberts, and Brandi Chastain, among others—all people from the soccer world whom I played against and who competed for spots to get into residency camp to train for the 1996 Summer Olympics.

Roberts was on the 1995 Women's World Cup team that had lost to the Norwegians. All newcomers were told that losing was not acceptable. This would be a year of hard work and revenge. DiCicco wanted us all to know that we wanted to win the Olympics. We were going to do whatever we needed to win!

Training camp was difficult. There were twenty-four or twenty-five spots for residency camp, with two floater spots. At the end of two weeks, Tony would post a list to tell us who was headed to camp. I honestly had no idea how I was doing—or if I was going to be on that list. I can remember walking to see the list and praying to God that whatever happens is for the best.

My whole body at the end of the two weeks was shouting with pain. From the big blisters on my feet to the pains in my neck from heading balls, I was sore all over. If I was going to make the list, the last thing that I wanted to do in front of everyone was shout for joy. On the flipside, I wanted to avoid crying if I didn't make the list.

As I walked toward the list—praying and trying to remain calm— I looked up and saw names that I expected to see, such as Mia Hamm, Michelle Akers, and all the other big-time veterans. Toward the bottom were the new names: Kate Sobrero, Brandi Chastain, Christie Pearce, Sara Whalen, Cindy Parlow. As I got to the bottom, there it was, second to last, my name in large print: DANIELLE GARRETT. I had made the cut as a floater.

I remained calm, although a subtle look of joy took over my face. Once I left the building and walked around the corner, I jumped up and down in jubilation. After I thanked God, I called my mom and told her.

"Mom! Mom! I am on the list. I do not know exactly what a floater is, but I am on the list and I am going to be given the opportunity to play with the best and compete with the best!" I exclaimed.

That is how my national team career started. I have not looked back since. To this day, I do all I can for soccer in America. Whether playing for my country, coaching kids in preschool or in college (even my own children), or being on the board of the athlete's council for the United States Soccer Federation, I hope to influence others in the same way that soccer has influenced my life.

In closing, I encourage you to read this book and enjoy the wonderful journey that has been the growth and development of the U.S. women's soccer team over the past twenty-five years. Clemente has compiled a wonderful account of this team's many joys, along with some disappointments, that will surely remain with you for years to come. He has also allowed young readers, especially girls, to read about female role models, in the hope that they too will become strong women that a future generation can look up to.

Danielle Fotopoulos played for the U.S. national team between 1996 and 2005, scoring sixteen goals in thirty-five appearances. She remains the National Collegiate Athletic Association's Division I all-time goals and assists leader and was on the team that won the 1999 Women's World Cup. Before retiring in 2007, she played three seasons for the Carolina Courage of the Women's United Soccer Association, scoring the winning goal in the 2002 championship game. She currently runs the Fotop Soccer Camps with her husband, George, former coach of the Louisiana State women's soccer team.

Acknowledgments

This book would not have been possible if not for a lot of caffeine—beverages both hot and cold—and quite a few late-night snacks to fuel me along the way (especially nachos and salsa). I have no regrets about losing many a night's sleep and many a Saturday afternoon working on this worthwhile project. No author, of course, can write a book without oodles of help. Although there are too many people to thank, I would like to single out a few.

First, I would like to thank my wonderful wife, Kate, who regularly left our apartment and created an atmosphere for me to write in peace and quiet despite the birth of our lovely daughter, Grace. I would also like to thank my parents, Franco and Rachele, and my sister, Paola, for their love and support throughout this long process.

I would also like to thank Aaron Heifetz, U.S. Soccer's director of communications for the women's team. He was always there to answer questions, put me in touch with players, and reply to my constant e-mails over the years. Without him and his office, this book would be missing a valuable piece, particularly when it comes to statistics.

J Hutcherson over at USSoccerPlayers.com deserves my gratitude for allowing me to cover such a great team and such a wonderful group of players.

Kudos to the staff at ISI Photos, especially John Todd, for helping me navigate the photo process that resulted in the great photography that made its way into the pages of this book.

Also a note of appreciation to my editor Stephen Ryan, who talked me back into writing this book after I had given up on the project during its early stages. His motivation, kind words, and experience turned this book from an idea into a reality. I would also like to thank the entire staff at Scarecrow Press, including Jayme Reed, who was part of this project every step of the way.

Finally, a big thank you to U.S. players, past and present, for allowing me to interview them and tell their incredible story. A special thanks to former soccer star Danielle Fotopoulos, who wrote the foreword to this book. Her experiences and kind words lend credibility to this project and give insight from one of this country's best players.

I would also like to thank everyone at Taylor Trade Publishing for publishing the second edition of this book, in particular Alyssa Johnson and Jehanne Schweitzer.

Introduction

What took place at the Rose Bowl in Pasadena under a sunny California sky on a July afternoon in 1999 remains this country's proudest soccer moment. More than ninety thousand fans—mostly screaming girls—occupied the stands, with another forty million watching on television, as the United States outlasted China on penalty kicks to win the World Cup. Outside the United States, the world treated the Women's World Cup with indifference. Although men's soccer powers such as Italy and Brazil also played at the tournament, they got little attention back home—similar to the way that typical American sports fans treat international soccer. In this case, however, American fans treated the tournament as a world-class event. Whereas foreign fans would never equate the skills of Mia Hamm to those of Diego Maradona, Americans were more than happy to worship Hamm as most international fans at the time revered Brazilian striker Ronaldo.

To most around the globe, soccer is a men's game. To many, the best players were men, although Americans finally embraced the world's game—after decades of trying—and redefined the sport as a "girls' game." This egalitarian view heaped on soccer was in large part due to Title IX of the Education Amendment Act. Signed into law by President Richard Nixon in 1972, it prohibited gender discrimination in any educational program or activity that was receiving federal money. Although sports were not the focus of the legislation, it was the one area that quickly bore visible fruit, culminating with the U.S. World Cup victory just seventeen years later. What emerged at the 1999 Women's World Cup was unprecedented in the history of American sports and international soccer. Fans came in all genders and sizes—many wearing red, white, and blue face paint and fitted pink jerseys with the name Hamm emblazoned on the back.

Working as a reporter, I was among these shrieking girls of all ages, accompanied in most cases by their SUV-driving moms and dads, when the United States played the first game of the 1999 Women's World Cup at Giants Stadium, about a thirty-minute drive from New York City. The earsplitting screaming, in a crowd composed almost entirely of white suburban families, filled the stands. Right before kickoff, the stadium, home to the NFL's New York Jets and Giants, was filled to the brim. The crowd chanted "USA! USA!" as the players walked out onto the lush, freshly laid sod. Soccer, I thought at the time, had finally made it as a sport in the United States—even though the country hosted the 1994 Men's World Cup to record crowds. Despite that feeling, I was wrong.

That 1999 victory faded away much like the infamous pet rock. To be honest, with the exception of the 2000 and 2004 Summer Olympics, my interest in women's soccer, like that of the country at large, had waned. I was too busy throwing myself into the men's game, and as a result, Hamm and her teammates took a backseat in my consciousness to the skills and antics of the U.S. men's national team and the weekly soap opera that is the English Premier League. That happened to the majority of American sports fans as well. Instead of watching soccer, most of them were enthralled by football and baseball.

In 2007, my interest in the women's game was renewed. I became so interested in the Women's World Cup in September 2007 that it changed my regular soccer-viewing habits. Instead of watching Serie A games from Italy on Sunday mornings—as I had my entire life—I demoted teams such as AC Milan and Napoli and promoted the women's tournament to my attention. I even passed up the classic Roma–Juventus match one Sunday morning in favor of Brazil–Australia.

This may sound like soccer heresy to traditional fans, but those who set their alarm clocks and crawled out of bed to watch the games beamed live from China at 5:00 AM were not at all disappointed by the skill and artistry that those female athletes displayed on the field. U.S. striker Abby Wambach's physical style and nonstop hustle introduced us all to a new era in the women's game. How many male players could endure constant pummeling by opposing defenders (like Wambach did in the United States' first-round match against North Korea), receiving eleven stitches to the head and returning to the game?

The mesmerizing skills of Brazilian striker Marta, for example, the female equivalent to Ronaldinho, were reminiscent of the beauty and skill made popular around the world for generations by her male countrymen. England striker Kelly Smith was also truly magnificent with the ball, serving up crisp passes to her teammates with flawless ease, much like David Beckham has done for over a decade for his country's men's team.

My first experience with women's soccer was in high school when I watched the Americans win the inaugural Women's World Cup in 1991 on tape delay—in Spanish! I still remember the United States finally winning an international soccer trophy and how no one seemed to notice. In 1999, I covered the Women's World Cup as a freelance sportswriter for the Scripps Howard News Service. During that magical three-week period, Hamm and her teammates put on a great display, caught the attention of a nation that has traditionally shunned soccer, and, for even a brief moment, made the world's game—and women's sports—a topic of conversation around water-coolers in offices across the country.

Two days after the United States defeated China on penalty kicks to win the tournament before a sold-out crowd at the Rose Bowl, I spent eleven hours following the team around New York as it made the rounds of the various morning and afternoon television talk shows. I found the players, particularly Julie Foudy and Brandi Chastain, to be the nicest group of athletes anyone could ever meet. They signed autographs for every single person and child who asked, gave advice to little boys and girls, and even took the time to answer questions from a pesky reporter like me.

Indeed, the 1999 World Cup title was the culmination of Title IX. Despite the strides made over the past thirty years and the popularity of the U.S. women's team, we are still not quite there when it comes to equality. Yes, females may have the same amount of opportunities in athletics at the levels of both high school and college,

xviii Introduction

but they still lack the same amount of respect that men's sports are given by television networks, newspapers, and society in general. As egalitarian as American society is, what is the message that we have sent young girls who want to grow up and be athletes? Maybe you can become a figure skater, participate at the Olympics as a gymnast, even become a basketball player, but that's about it. And if you're really interested in sports, then maybe you can get a job working as a sideline reporter covering football.

The truth is that ever since the 1999 Women's World Cup, some pathbreakers suffered ideas of grandeur when it came to the marketing of women's soccer. Instead of looking at that tournament as a one-off, women's soccer advocates thought the entire country was ready to embrace a new sport. It wasn't.

The Women's United Soccer Association, a league created after the 1999 tournament, failed in 2003 under a mountain of debt and empty stadiums. In 2008, as the country battled an economic recession some compared to the Great Depression, a new league was born. Women's Professional Soccer hopes to pick up where the Women's United Soccer Association left off—and, this time, succeed. The jury is still out on what the outcome will be and whether the league will be a viable, moneymaking operation.

Sports fans in general, mostly men, grumble that women's sports are just not exciting or appealing enough to warrant their attention. The Women's World Cup and Olympic soccer tournament, which both evolved into marquee sporting events over the past decade, are perfect examples of females competing at the highest levels. The games are entertaining and steadily catching up to the level of men's soccer. Some 18 million Americans currently play soccer at some level, 7.5 million of which are girls or adult women. The future of the U.S. Women's national team, a trailblazer in a sport not popular with a majority of Americans, is bright as a new generation of young ladies are being groomed to someday, in the not-so-distant future, win another World Cup.

1

Top of the World

A strange Thanksgiving dinner took place in 1991 during the late afternoon of November 28 in the southern Chinese city of Guangzhou, formerly known as Canton, just a few hours away by train from the sprawling urban center of Hong Kong. Gathered at the table inside the White Swan Hotel, a sleek and elegant twenty-five-floor building on the banks of the mud-colored Pearl River, was a group of young women in the process of making American—if not global—sports history. Some players gazed out the window in amazement at the skyscrapers as the city of six million people went about their day. Some joked with one another. Others just ate.

Among the women sitting at the table was Michelle Akers-Stahl, whose bushy blonde mane resembled that of a lion and whose bulging biceps and muscular legs were comparable to those of any professional male soccer player. In some ways, Akers-Stahl was much tougher than any man. Not only had she reached the status of best female soccer player on the planet, but she had also blazed a trail for women to play the world's most popular sport in a country where it had traditionally toiled in obscurity. Akers-Stahl, only twenty-five, was a three-time All-American at Shorecrest High School in Seattle who went on to play for the University of Central Florida. She won the Hermann Trophy, given to the country's best female player, in 1988 and had been part of the U.S. team from its inception, in 1985.

As her teammates munched on a traditional meal of turkey drowned in gravy, Akers-Stahl sat there, playing with her food as she occasionally stared down at a large red bandage placed around her right knee to protect a deep cut. The bandage had been the result of a freak injury suffered two months earlier after she had accidentally come into contact with a sharp sprinkler hidden amid a patch of overgrown grass. Now she and her teammates were a game away from glory at the inaugural Women's World Championship. In fact, the turkey dinner growing cold before Akers-Stahl was the last thing on her mind. Instead, she was focused on the next day's championship game against Norway. A lot was on the line. The winner would be crowned the first-ever women's world soccer champion. "We had played well the entire tournament, but now we knew we had to beat one of the best teams in the world if we wanted to make history. We knew it was not going to be easy. We knew that we had to beat the best to be the best," said Akers.[1]

Sixty-one years after FIFA, soccer's world governing body, staged the first World Cup for men in 1930, the first world championship for women was launched in the fall of 1991. The brainchild of FIFA President Joaõ Havelange, the groundbreaking tournament was held in China without much hype. The only corporate sponsor to sign on was M&M's candy, a far cry from the dozens of advertisers who had traditionally clamored for ad space at the male version of the World Cup.

However small the tournament was, it was a sign that the women's game had finally arrived. Well, not really. FIFA decided that games would last only eighty minutes (two forty-minute halves instead of the usual forty-five) because it was under the misguided impression that women did not have the stamina to play a full ninety minutes like men. Women's soccer, although tactically naïve compared to the more-established men's game, did have something that the male version did not have. For starters, it was open to a greater number of scoring chances—and, therefore, more goals—because players were not afraid to take risks or embark on offensive forays, sometimes as a liability to their team's defense. However, women played at a much slower pace—with the exception of a few players, like Akers-Stahl—and were more prone to injuries because of constant collisions with one another. But the collisions were more a result of sloppy play, rather than the intentional fouling of an opponent, which had and still remains an unfortunate staple of the men's game. Women's soccer was relatively new as a global phenomenon. Out of eighty-six nations with women's national teams, only forty-four attempted to qualify for the 1991 World Championship. The U.S. team, which was first formed by the U.S. Soccer Federation six years earlier, had been blazing a trail that finally led to a shot at a world title. The growth of female soccer players in this country was a direct result of Title IX, signed into law on June 23, 1972, by President Richard Nixon. Title IX of the 1972 Education Amendments Act prohibited discrimination on the basis of gender at institutions such as high schools and colleges that received any federal funding. The act was intended to give women equal access to professional careers such as law and medicine. Although women did receive greater access to those fields of study, they also began to play sports in larger numbers. By 1991, American women represented 40 percent of the country's fifteen million registered soccer players. In 1971, the number of women who competed in collegiate sports was 29,977; by 1997, it was 128,209.[2] Whereas soccer had become a staple of U.S. collegiate athletic programs in the mid-1970s, most countries did not field a women's squad, not even Argentina, which is known for its successful men's national teams of all age ranges.

After the United States Soccer Federation (USSF) announced that it was putting together a women's national team, Anson Dorrance (photo 1.1), a legend in college soccer circles after coaching both the men's team and the women's team at the University of North Carolina (UNC), applied for the job of head coach. The federation told Dorrance that he was not qualified for the position. At the time, Dorrance did not possess any experience coaching in a USSF-sanctioned tournament and, as a result, could not be considered for the job, despite his years of success with the Tar Heels. Dorrance was fiery, with wavy black hair and an angular jaw. He wanted to win. Above all, he wanted the U.S. coaching job. Dorrance never hid that truth, but the powers that be at the USSF did not like his aggressive attitude. They viewed him as abrasive and combative.

Dorrance had previously tangled with the federation's administrators—many of whom were lawyers with little soccer know-how—and he made no bones about wanting to get involved in the

Photo 1.1.   U.S. coach Anson Dorrance works the sidelines during a North Carolina game. (Credit: ISI Photos)

decision-making process concerning player development if he were ever to be named coach. For Dorrance, there was no way that he would be micromanaged by a bunch of lawyers. "Anson was an abrasive combination of politically incorrect and noisy. The administration at the time wasn't sophisticated enough to see the potential in that," admitted Chuck Blazer, who served as the USSF's executive vice president at the time.[3]

Instead, the USSF went with Mike Ryan as the team's first coach. The USSF funded the squad on a shoestring budget, and Ryan would later complain that the federation had not reimbursed him $1,000 in expenses during a span of six months.[4] The Irish-born Ryan coached the team at the Mundialito, a World Cup precursor, held in the town of Jesolo, in northern Italy, in the summer of 1985. The Italian Soccer Federation had invited the Americans, and it was the first time that the United States would get a chance to play against another national team.

The ill-prepared team only had a week to get ready for the competition, and it held a three-day camp at the University of Long Island's C. W. Post campus in suburban New York City. The players were housed in a dorm complex that included a group of giggling high school cheerleaders who practiced at all hours of the day and night, and they were given men's soccer uniforms without any letters or numbers on them. The players were forced to go to a local sporting goods store to have the letters and numbers ironed on the day before their scheduled flight. The players flew a charter plane out of New York, and once in Italy, the team was pressed into action. The players landed in Milan and traveled nearly five hours by bus to the tiny picturesque town of Jesolo. On August 18, 1985, the United States made its debut—a 1–0 loss to Italy. Three days later, Akers-Stahl scored the United States' first-ever goal in an eventual 2–2 tie against Denmark. The Americans gained only one point and finished the tournament a disappointing 0–3–1. Following the three losses, Ryan was fired.

In the spring of 1986, the USSF invited a number of coaches to Dallas to audition for several coaching jobs, including the one to fill the void left by Ryan. Among those invited was Dorrance, who at age thirty-five was the youngest candidate on the list. Of course, he still wanted the U.S. coaching job but felt like he had little chance. After the test, which consisted of coaching and analyzing several games, a cocky Dorrance told Blazer, "Chuck, give me the job because I am going to win."[5] Dorrance got the job.

Dorrance was born on April 9, 1951, in Bombay, India, the son of an American oil businessman. He spent most of his childhood moving from one country to another. Of all the places he lived, three had helped fuel Dorrance's love for the sport. One was the city of Addis Ababa, Ethiopia, where Dorrance met his future wife, M'Liss Gary, the daughter of a U.S. Air Force attaché living in the country at the time. The other places were Kenya, where Dorrance's love for soccer blossomed, and Switzerland, where he attended boarding school at a place called Villa St. Jean International School, in the city of Fribourg. He eventually moved to the United States and attended UNC. He was given a spot on the men's soccer team as a walk-on and eventually earned three-time All-Atlantic Coast Conference honors. He graduated in 1974 and married M'Liss later that year.

Dorrance, after taking advice from his father, attended UNC's law school but dropped out in 1976 after his former coach, Marvin

Allen, convinced him that he should take over as UNC's men's soccer coach. Dorrance eagerly accepted. In 1979, Dorrance's duties grew to include the newly established women's team. In a two-year span, Dorrance guided the Lady Tar Heels to a championship: the 1981 Association for Intercollegiate Athletics for Women title. When Dorrance had taken over the women's team, the NCAA (National Collegiate Athletic Association) did not have a women's soccer championship. Dorrance, along with University of Colorado coach Chris Lidstone, thus proposed the idea to the Association for Intercollegiate Athletics for Women, which embraced it. The NCAA finally recognized women's soccer as an intercollegiate sport worthy of a national championship. Dorrance's teams dominated the game from that point on. His teams won every championship from 1982 to 1984 and again from 1986 to 1994. The Lady Tar Heels, under Dorrance, would go on to win nineteen out of twenty-five national championships contested.

As U.S. coach, Dorrance's mission appeared simple—guide the team to North American dominance. Not a tough task when considering that only a handful of nations who played in the North and Central American region even fielded women's teams. The best of the bunch in 1986 was Canada. Beat its team and regional supremacy would be achieved. That same year, Dorrance wrote a letter to his players, saying that he was going to put a newfound emphasis on physical fitness. He knew that the key to success was to have players with athletic abilities superior to their opponents'. "If you don't come in fit, I will cut you!" the letter sternly warned.[6]

Cut he did. On the first day of training camp, Dorrance cut goalkeeper Barbara Wickstrand because she was out of shape and unprepared for the physical toll that her body would take as a result of his demanding training regimen. Dorrance knew that to succeed on the national team level, he would need the same tools that made him such a great college coach. The first was recruiting and his knack for eyeing outstanding young talent. Thanks to his UNC player pool and scouting reports from other collegiate coaches, Dorrance was all but guaranteed a steady flow of players.

His second tool was his emphasis on competitiveness. Dorrance believed that a physically fit player was also one who would perform better. He knew from his experience coaching men—and women—that female players exhibited shyness when it came to competing against others. At UNC, Dorrance learned that women who displayed an aggressive desire to win were the ones who succeeded most: "I knew that women had the same desire to win as men. The way to do that was to create a competitive aura as well as an atmosphere which focused on relationships. In that way, players would play aggressively and also have a sense of family off the field."[7]

Physical fitness would also go a long way in helping the United States dominate the field regionally. Dorrance's first game on the U.S. bench saw his team play Canada on July 7, 1986, in Blaine, Minnesota. He started five UNC players—including April Heinrichs (see p. 8), who would eventually be named team captain and emerge as one of the best players on the roster. The Americans won 2–0. Two days later, the Americans beat Canada again, 3–0. That summer, the United States was again invited to the Mundialito in Italy and finished with a 3–1 record with victories over China, Brazil, and Japan. Not bad for a team that did not even exist just twelve months earlier and had won no games at the previous year's tournament.

With talk that FIFA was planning to stage a Women's World Championship—chauvinistically refusing to call it a World Cup— Dorrance knew that he had to get his players more games against established powers such as Norway, which formed its national team in 1978 and was widely considered the best in the world. Dorrance spent most of 1987 scouting the U.S. Under-19 (U-19) women's national team pool. In the summer of that year, during a camp in Marquette, Michigan, Dorrance spotted two sixteen-year-olds: Julie Foudy and Kristine Lilly, players who would become regulars on the team. A phone call from a friend led Dorrance to a youth tournament in Louisiana to scout a fourteen-year-old named Mia Hamm. "The team kicks off, a girl passes the ball to the right about 30 yards and I see this skinny brunette take off like she had been shot out of a cannon," Dorrance recalled of seeing Hamm play for the first time.[8]

Dorrance was impressed. A year later, Hamm joined the national team, where she became a starter. It was the addition of Hamm, Foudy, and Lilly, who the older players called "The Kids," that led Dorrance to the radical plan of injecting youth players onto his team. From that point on, Dorrance mined the nation's suburban soccer fields for players whom he could recruit and shape. The move to include teenagers on a team of mostly college students and recent graduates was a big gamble.

Dorrance ran the risk of pitting adults against teenagers and ruining the confidence of younger players who were just starting out.

APRIL HEINRICHS

April Heinrichs was one of the first female athletes to play for the U.S. team. A pioneer of the program, Heinrichs captained the team that captured the inaugural Women's World Cup, in 1991. With thirty-eight goals in forty-seven appearances for the United States, Heinrichs, a midfielder, became the first female inducted into the National Soccer Hall of Fame; she was bestowed the honor in 1998.

A 1986 graduate of the University of North Carolina, Heinrichs excelled at the National Collegiate Athletic Association (NCAA) level and was named National Player of the Year twice, while earning All-American honors three times in the process. During her four years at Chapel Hill, the Tar Heels won three NCAA titles. In 1990, she compiled an 8–6–1 record as coach and proceeded to amass a 56–40–7 record in charge of the women's team at the University of Maryland. She earned Atlantic Coast Conference Coach of the Year honors in 1995 after guiding the program to its first NCAA Tournament berth.

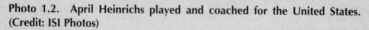

Photo 1.2. April Heinrichs played and coached for the United States. (Credit: ISI Photos)

Heinrichs served as head coach of the University of Virginia from 1996 to 2000, recording an impressive 52–27–7 record in leading the program to four straight NCAA Tournament appearances. Her best season at the helm was in 1999, when she led the school's women's team to a 13–10 record and a tournament appearance.

Her success led to an appointment as assistant coach of the U.S. women's squad in 1995. She was named head coach in 2000. Heinrichs's tenure, however, was not without criticism. She was often accused of failing to get results from the players, although the United States did capture the gold medal at the 2004 Summer Games in Athens with her on the bench. Heinrichs compiled an 87–17–20 record during her five years with the U.S. team. She resigned in February 2005 to become a consultant for U.S. Soccer.

In 2005, Heinrichs was named head coach of the women's team at the University of California–Irvine but resigned later that year to take a position with the U.S. Olympic Committee.

Appearances: 47

Goals: 38

Dorrance did not care. He relished the chance to pit a player with the raw talent of Hamm against the likes of Norway. The Americans had scheduled two games in China, and Dorrance named Hamm, Foudy, and Lilly to the roster.

The three teenagers made a name for themselves. Hamm and Lilly both started in their debuts, on August 3 against China, where the Americans blanked their opponent 2–0. Ten days later, the United States tied China 1–1, with Hamm and Lilly starting again. Lilly scored for the United States. Foudy, however, had failed to prove to Dorrance that she could keep up with her teammates and was thus relegated to the bench. Foudy would not become a starter until 1988. "The team finally had a certain edge to it. They were playing as a unit," said Dorrance.[9]

The move to swap maturity for teen potential angered many at the USSF, who thought that some of this country's most talented college players were being left off the team. Nonsense, Dorrance responded, and he continued with his plan. "When you pick a lot of your own players for the team, the only way you can justify that is by winning," he said.[10] Instead, the team, which featured mostly UNC players, lost. They lost to New Zealand and Taiwan in 1987, and Dorrance's record since deciding to replace experience with youth stood at a respectable 7–5–3.

The USSF did not fire Dorrance. Instead, it took shots at him every chance it got. At the 1990 Olympic Sports Festival, held in Minneapolis–St. Paul, the USSF organized a tournament between Dorrance's team, the U.S. U-19 squad (which largely featured players that Dorrance had passed on), and two teams made up of the best remaining players. Dorrance's team won all its games, including a 2–0 win over the U-19 squad. Following the game, some of the U-19 players made it known to federation officials that they believed that they were better than some of Dorrance's benchwarmers.

In a rematch with the U-19 team, Dorrance decided to prove that he was right, and he started seven of his reserves. Dorrance's team won 10–0. When the game ended, Dorrance was relieved. A feeling of satisfaction came over him. He had finally silenced his critics. When USSF secretary-general Keith Walker set foot in the locker room after the game, Dorrance thought he was going to get a hug. Instead, he got a tongue-lashing. "What is this I hear that you've left some of the best American players off the team?" barked Walker, referring to the players who had lost the game.[11]

Dorrance felt betrayed. He had worked hard to put together a competitive team that was actually showing results, and all the federation cared about was the feelings of a few players who had been left out. Dorrance felt vulnerable, like he could be fired at any moment. He was left twisting in the wind, although he had enough fire in his belly to lash back: "I was incredulous, and finally I said, 'What game were you watching?'"[12]

Walker made it clear that he did not want the Americans to lose against Germany in an upcoming friendly. Dorrance did not disappoint. With a confident demeanor, a competitive roster, and an effective plan, Dorrance watched his team mow down opponents faster and more effectively than the lawnmowers that prepped the playing field. A month later in Blaine, the United States defeated Germany 3–0, with Walker watching from the stands. That summer the United States also defeated England, the Soviet Union, and Norway (twice). Dorrance's plan to transform his players into a cohesive unit was coming along nicely. He had finally become a competent coach in the eyes of many at the USSF. The federation soon realized that Dorrance was qualified for the job after all.

The Women's World Championship qualifying tournament took place in Haiti in April 1991. Hotel accommodations were abysmal. Electricity was unreliable and hot water scarce. Things were so bad that some players bathed in the hotel swimming pool just because that had become the only reliable place to find clean water. The Americans easily qualified, scoring a staggering forty-nine goals over five games. Now, all that stood in their way were the world's best teams, and Dorrance could finally show everyone that his squad was a dominant global power, despite an annual budget of just $175,000.

The World Championship, which featured twelve teams, was supposed to be a subdued affair. FIFA did not expect much from the tournament, but someone had forgotten to tell the organizers and the fans. The Chinese people came out in droves to watch the games. The excitement that swept across the country paralleled that of any World Cup. The atmosphere was electric, and stadiums filled with thousands of fans. The United States was placed in Group B, along with Sweden, Brazil, and Japan. A "tough group," according to Dorrance, but "not an impossible one" to advance out of.[13]

Dorrance knew that the United States had never defeated Sweden, but he expected to get points off countries that he had defeated before, such as Brazil and Japan. The Americans stayed in Guangzhou, although a diet of ox, dog, and cat was not to the players' liking. The team survived mostly on Snickers bars, available to them in bulk because Mars/M&M's was the tournament's sponsor. The players spent their $10 per diem meal stipend on packaged snacks. Despite the lack of a good diet, Dorrance tried to rally his players and lift their morale by keeping them focused on the ultimate prize of being crowned world champions. "How many people ever get the chance to be the best in the world at something?" Dorrance told his players.[14]

The Americans did compete like world champions. On November 17, the United States played its first game against Sweden at Yinh Dong Stadium in the city of Panyu before fourteen thousand fans. The United States jumped out to a 1–0 lead in the forty-third minute with Carin Jennings, who faked two defenders and slid a shot past goalkeeper Elisabeth Leidinge at the near post.

The United States doubled its lead when Jennings's shot bounced off the crossbar and hit the ground on the goal line. Heinrichs kicked in the rebound for the goal. In the sixty-second minute, Hamm made it 3–0 when she beat Leidinge with a twenty-five-foot rocket. Sweden had pressured the U.S. defense in spurts during the first half, even coming close to scoring, but its best effort was thwarted by defender Shannon Higgins, who cleared a loose ball off the line. In the second half, however, Sweden mounted a late rally. With thirteen minutes left to play, Lena Videkull knocked in a loose ball past goalkeeper Mary Harvey for the goal. The Swedes scored a second unanswered goal in the seventy-first minute with Ingrid Johansson off a forty-yard shot. The Americans staved off the Swedes in the final nineteen minutes to pull off a hard-fought 3–2 win. "I thought we were lucky to have dodged all those bullets. I was very pleased that we scored three goals, but we are still somewhat naïve. When you are up by three goals, we shouldn't have been as nervous as we were," said Dorrance.[15]

Two days later, the United States took to the field, again in Panyu, against Brazil before 15,500 spectators. Heinrichs put the Americans in the lead after twenty-three minutes off a fifteen-yard shot delivered from Jennings. After a series of missed chances, Jennings made it 2–0 with five minutes left in the first half off a left-footed shot that hit the top corner of the net. Jennings scored her third goal of the tournament in the forty-third minute off a beautifully placed pass from Heinrichs. Akers-Stahl scored a minute later, putting the ball in the net following a scramble in front of the goalmouth for a 4–0 halftime lead. Hamm scored a goal—her second of the tournament—with fifteen minutes left in the game to cap off the 5–0 win. "I think our performance was the result of being much more relaxed than in the first game. Getting the Sweden game out of the way was a tremendous release," said Heinrichs.[16]

The Americans, with two wins in two games, clinched a berth to the quarterfinals with a game left to play in the first round. On November 21, the United States took on Japan in New Plaza Stadium in Foshan. The game meant nothing to either side. The United States had already qualified for the next round, and Japan, which had recorded two losses, was out of the tournament. Japan was no match. The Americans, under Dorrance's stern gaze, played like they needed the win. Akers-Stahl made it 1–0 after twenty-two minutes off a twenty-yard shot that found the back of the net. Wendy Gebauer scored in the thirty-ninth minute to make it 2–0.

Akers-Stahl tallied her third goal of the tournament with five minutes left in the first half, when she stuffed the ball into the net from close range off a pass from Jennings. Dorrance, feeling as though the game was secured at halftime, took Akers-Stahl and Jennings out to rest them for the next match. The Americans, 3–0 winners over Japan, won the group, scoring eleven goals and giving up only two. At the same time, in Panyu, Sweden defeated Brazil 2–0 to finish second and also clinch a berth to the elimination round. In the other first round finishes, China and Norway qualified out of Group A and Germany and Italy out of Group C. Denmark in Group A and Chinese Taipei in Group C also qualified, as the two teams with the best third-place records. As a result, the Americans were paired against Chinese Taipei, a relatively weak opponent. The other quarterfinal matchups were as follows: Germany against Denmark, China versus Sweden, and Norway taking on Italy.

On November 25, half a world away from where Dorrance and his team was training, UNC faced Wisconsin for the NCAA Division I title. The nine former and current UNC players on the U.S. team begged Dorrance to phone the press box in Chapel Hill for regular updates during the game. As some players sat and others anxiously paced the halls of their hotel in Guangzhou, Dorrance obliged, regularly making long-distance calls to get the latest score. Dorrance had no problem leaving his beloved UNC team in the competent hands of his assistant coach Bill Palladino. UNC had reached the final without Dorrance for much of the season and was now on the verge of winning the NCAA title with him in China.

When Dorrance called one last time, the voice on the other end of the line gave him the final score: UNC 3, Wisconsin 1. The players were elated. UNC was again the best women's college team in the country. Dorrance had won another title without even being there. Now he wanted to cap the whole thing off by becoming a world champion.

Although Dorrance was enthusiastic that his team had won another title, he tried to remain focused on what was going on around him in China. On November 24, the United States took on Chinese Taipei in Foshan before twelve thousand fans. The Americans showed no mercy against their weak opponents, creating chance upon chance with every passing minute. Akers-Stahl, with the help of her speed and physical dominance, put the United States in the lead after just eight minutes, doubled the score twenty-one minutes later, and completed her hat trick in the thirty-third minute. Foudy scored five minutes later to make it 4–0 at halftime.

The Americans made it look easy. An unstoppable Akers-Stahl did not stop there. She scored her fourth goal of the game on a penalty kick in the forty-fourth minute to put the United States ahead 5–0. She then scored again, this time from a diving header, four minutes later for what had become a rout. In the end, the Americans put together an impressive 7–0 victory. Dorrance's smile afterward told the whole story. He was happy with the United States' performance and, for the first time, could breathe a sigh of relief: "I feel very good about the way our team is coming together now."[17]

Akers-Stahl emerged as the team leader and was now the tournament's top scorer with eight goals. "It was probably her best finishing game ever. She had some remarkable goals," Dorrance bragged when Akers-Stahl's name came up during a news conference after the game.[18]

The United States now faced Germany, which had defeated Denmark 2–1. Sweden, which eliminated hosts China 1–0, would have to play Norway in the other semifinal. Norway had defeated Italy 3–2 in overtime.

The American media, minus a few exceptions (such as *Soccer America* and *USA Today*), had largely ignored the tournament until this point but now began to jump on the U.S. bandwagon. As the Americans advanced deeper into the tournament, the *New York Times* and the *Washington Post* immediately dispatched stringers to China, whereas *Sports Illustrated* sent a correspondent who had never covered a soccer game. Now that the United States was in the semifinals, newsrooms and some fans back home took notice.

Dorrance and his players were on the verge of making history. Dorrance, however, preferred the lack of media coverage: Few reporters and sparse coverage—with the exception of the Chinese press—allowed him to work in relative anonymity. There were no journalists to second-guess his decisions; therefore, he could go ahead with his plans without any criticism.

On November 27, the United States took on Germany in the semifinals at Guangdong Provincial Stadium in Guangzhou before fifteen thousand fans. During the three-day gap following the rout of Chinese Taipei, Dorrance was cautious about getting overexcited with his team's prospects of winning the tournament. His attitude of taking it one game at a time rubbed off on the players. True, the United States—and Akers-Stahl—was a formidable force, but Dorrance was happier praising his opponents in public than talking about his own players. Despite that approach, Dorrance could not overlook another reality: His team was 4–0, outscoring opponents a staggering 18–2 over those four games. Germany, which was also 4–0, had outscored opponents 11–2 and featured a hard-hitting defense and a well-organized midfield. The fear at the USSF was that the United States had finally met its match. "Germany is an outstanding team with a great tradition. I think they are going to be a formidable opponent," said Dorrance.[19]

In reality, the Americans were a lot more talented than the Germans. They were stronger and faster at virtually every position, and it showed once the game got underway. The fans in attendance may not have known it, but they were in for one of the most exciting games of the competition. The United States' aggressive play resulted in the Germans repeatedly turning over the ball. As a result, Jennings was able to put the United States ahead after just ten minutes, taking advantage of an errant back pass by the German defense to knock the ball into the net. Jennings made it 2–0 in the twenty-first minute when she took a pass from Hamm in the midfield and beat goalkeeper Marion Isbert from twenty-five yards out. Eight minutes later, Jennings took advantage of another defensive mishap—scoring a hat trick and tallying her sixth goal of the tournament—to make it 3–0. "She shreds defenses. She absolutely shreds them," Dorrance said following the game.[20]

Although Jennings knew that her teammates were playing their best game of the tournament, she made sure they were cautious in the back and followed through on their passes: "Even though we were up three goals at the half, we knew we couldn't relax. We knew we had to concentrate. You can't relax against Germany," she said.[21]

The Germans did put a scare into Dorrance and his players. Heidi Mohr scored with eight minutes left in the first half, but the Americans went ahead 4–1 in the fifty-fourth minute when Jennings scored off her own rebound following a perfectly executed cross from Heinrichs. "We like to play high pressure ball. We forced them to make mistakes," said Heinrichs.[22]

The physical nature of the game started to take its toll on both sides. A series of sliding tackles and rough play made it the most grueling match of the tournament. In the end, Chilean referee Salvador Imperatore Marcone would hand out just two yellow cards—with one going to Akers-Stahl in the second half—in what had been a punishing match. When both sides were not kicking and knocking each other to the ground, they were scoring goals. Germany netted a second goal with Bettina Weigmann in the sixty-first minute, but Heinrichs responded with another tally of her own—her fifth of the competition—with six minutes left to play to make it 5–2. When the final whistle blew, the American players celebrated. The crowd, which had backed both teams at various points of the game, applauded. The Americans were in the final.

The United States was pitted against Norway, which had trounced Sweden 4–1 earlier in the day in Panyu, in the title match. Even Dorrance, always a believer in his players' abilities, was in shock over reaching the final.

"Right now, I'm a little numb. I still feel the tension of knowing that Germany, as good as they are, had the ability to come back. I'm sure the reality of playing in a world championship game will sink in later tonight," he said.[23]

Despite Dorrance's compliments, Germany coach Gero Bisanz launched into a tirade on how rough the Americans had played. The Americans took the criticism in stride. After all, they were playing for a shot at the world title, not the Germans.

Both the American players and the Norwegians stayed at the White Swan Hotel in the three days preceding the November 30 final at Tianhe Stadium in Guangzhou. Although the Americans were upset with the arrangement (it would have been inconceivable that two men's national teams would share a hotel in the days before such a big game), the move was aimed at reducing costs. In the end, the American players agreed that staying in the same hotel was best. The comfortable accommodations and a Thanksgiving meal were an improvement over the candy bars that the players used to sustain themselves over most of the competition.

The United States' starting lineup on the day of the final featured six Tar Heels: Hamm, Lilly, Heinrichs, Carla Werden (who later took her married name, Overbeck), Linda Hamilton, and Shannon Higgins. Another UNC graduate, Birthe Hegstad, was on the other side, and she was named a starting midfielder for Norway. Dorrance tried to relax his players, reassuring them that they had the skill and character to win against such a tough opponent. They had defeated Germany in a hard-fought contest just days earlier. Surely a victory over Norway was possible. Dorrance gathered the players in the locker room before kickoff and began his pregame speech by reading them a poem written by one of their mothers—who exactly, he kept to himself. The poem read, "Yes, you've arrived, the goal is right / But the cup is not all, let's get this right." The poem ended, "You're a woman, of course, and a champion, my dear." Signed: "Mom."[24] It was not until after the game that the coach told Higgins that it was her mother who had written the poem.

When Dorrance finished reading the poem aloud, many of the players became emotional. Tears streamed down their faces. The poem put into words all the feelings of such a big game. Sentiment had finally reached an all-time high. All the players had to do now was turn that passion into a win.

Dorrance had intentionally not revealed whose mother had written the poem because he wanted each player to believe that it might have been her own mother who penned such inspirational words. Before the game, none other than Brazilian legend Pelé took to the field, making his way down the line. He greeted the players before the national anthems were played. The game finally came to a start when referee Vadim Zhuk of Bulgaria blew the whistle and the sixty-three thousand fans in attendance made their presence known with a huge roar. The large crowd had surprised not only FIFA but both teams as well. What was supposed to be a tournament played before sparse crowds had instead captivated a nation. The Chinese public had embraced women's soccer with both arms. The least that both teams could do now was repay them with a well-played, highly entertaining game.

The Americans, tired and battered from their brutal semifinal against Germany, appeared slow in the early going. They knew that they had to play smart against the Norwegians, but Dorrance expected the same high level of pressure to win balls in the midfield and create scoring chances up top, as in earlier games. Indeed, every Norway turnover was a chance for the U.S. attack to create a scoring opportunity. Akers-Stahl scored in the twentieth minute off a header—following a Higgins free kick—that beat goalkeeper Reidun Seth for the 1–0 lead. Norway responded eight minutes later to tie the score on a similar play when Linda

Medalen, Norway's top scorer, headed in her sixth goal of the tournament.

At halftime, Higgins ran up to Dorrance and gave him a laundry list of everything that was going wrong. True, the United States had the "triple-edged sword," a phrase used by the Chinese media to describe the three-pronged offense of Akers-Stahl, Jennings, and Heinrichs. The first time that all three players had scored in a game was a good omen—it came in July 1990 in a 4–0 win over Norway in Winnipeg, Canada. In 1990, those three players accounted for eighteen of the team's twenty-six goals over six games. Dorrance knew that the trio could do it again in China.

Despite those standout numbers, Dorrance also knew that his players were tired. He had his back to the wall. He refused to share all of Higgins's concerns with the rest of the team for fear that the little optimism that was there would vanish. Dorrance shared some of his concerns with the players in the dressing room but made no substitutions. He couldn't. The team had no depth. The bench players were too inexperienced for such a big game. Putting any of them in would have meant surrendering to the astute Norwegians.

The second half was similar to the first forty minutes of play—intense and physically exhausting. The U.S. team was breaking down, both physically and mentally at just the wrong time, while Norway was able to push the ball farther into the American half. Dorrance wanted his players to move on. He continued to gamble and made no subs. Instead, he gave the exhausted players a pep talk whenever the ball came close to the sidelines, anything to inject some motivation and confidence into their play. Akers-Stahl and her teammates had to use what little adrenaline they had left to maintain their composure. The fans who packed the stands chanted incessantly as the game headed for overtime. Suddenly, the crowd, which had rooted on both sides, took an unusual pro-American tone midway through the second half. Maybe it was Norway's dull and uninspiring play that turned the crowd against the team. Either way, the Americans felt uplifted.

The Norwegians had traditionally employed an unattractive but often effective style of kicking long balls to their strikers in an effort to create goals. Playing the ball at midfield with fluid passes and one-on-one challenges was Dorrance's style, and it made for both effective and beautiful soccer. With the crowd cheering on the American squad, the players fed off that support, and Dorrance used every chance he could to shout orders from the bench.

With only three minutes left in the game, Norwegian defender Tina Svensson misplayed the ball back to Seth. Akers-Stahl used what little speed she had left to pounce on the ball, intercepting it, and dribbling around the hapless Seth. Akers-Stahl then deposited the ball into the empty net with her right foot for the 2–1 winner. It was the only real mistake that the Norwegian defense made all evening, but Akers-Stahl, ever the opportunistic striker, took advantage of the error to tally her tournament-leading tenth goal. Dorrance and the bench erupted into cheers, and the crowd joined in.

"Not to take anything away from Michelle, she's the top scorer in this tournament, but the odds of a player of that caliber, such as Svensson, making that kind of mistake are remote. [Akers-Stahl] jumped on that chance," said Dorrance.[25] Akers-Stahl even earned praise from Pelé, who said, "I like her because she is intelligent, has presence of mind and is often in the right position. She's fantastic."[26]

The final few minutes felt like an eternity. The Americans maintained possession and resisted the urge to foul the Norwegians when they had the ball, in an effort not to give their opponents any real chance to score. Then the final whistle blew. Of the remaining few minutes, Dorrance said afterward, "I felt like I was creating diamonds in my lower intestines from the pressure."[27]

The Americans had won their fifth straight game, outscoring all opponents 23–4. More important, for the first time, the United States had done the impossible and won an international soccer tournament. No American men's team of any age level had been able to win a World Cup. The women finally had. "When they start listing world champions in women's soccer, the United States is at the top of that list. We feel both lucky and privileged to be the first champion of women's soccer," said Dorrance.[28]

Afterward, the players were greeted in their locker room with a table filled with platters of fruit and champagne bottles. The players indulged themselves, happily shaking the bottles and spraying each other with the bubbly in unabashed jubilation. On the team bus, the players danced and sang as they made their way across the darkened streets of Guangzhou. Pedestrians applauded them whenever the bus stopped as the players belted out the chorus from the song "We Are the Champions!"

However, what was the start of a global women's soccer revolution had gone practically unnoticed back in the United States. Hamm recalled, "Prior to leaving for China, we would tell people that we were going to the World Cup, and they'd smile and say, 'Uh that's nice.' But they didn't really have a clue as to what we were talking about."[29]

On December 3, when the travel-weary players walked into the International Arrivals Building at John F. Kennedy Airport in New York, there were only a few people at the gate to greet them, including three reporters and several USSF officials. Swiss Air staffers lined up and handed the players roses as they made their way into the terminal. USSF officials tried to get some local girls to attend the homecoming party but were unable to get them out of school.

"There were no TV crews or fans waiting for us at the airport when we returned, just several friends and U.S. Soccer representatives," said Hamm.[30] One of them was the U.S. men's coach at the time, Bora Milutinovic, who offered Dorrance his congratulations. "I'm very happy for the women's team. I am happy for all of American soccer," said Milutinovic, who was staying in New York in preparation for the 1994 World Cup qualifying draw at Madison Square Garden.[31]

There were no parades. No celebrations. No anything. The players got zero endorsements. No paychecks for their effort. No fame. Just joy and love for a game. Indeed, the Americans had finally won a world title, but few people—even hard-core soccer fans—had noticed or cared. "I hope what we've done will prove that we are a developing soccer nation," said Dorrance.[32]

His hope would grow leaps and bounds within the decade.

NOTES

1. Interview, June 19, 1999.
2. National Collegiate Athletic Association.
3. Tim Crothers, *The Man Watching: A Biography of Anson Dorrance, the Unlikely Architect of the Greatest College Sports Dynasty Ever* (Ann Arbor, MI: Sports Media Group, 2006), 149.
4. Jere Longman, *The Girls of Summer: The U.S. Women's Soccer Team and How It Changed the World* (New York: HarperCollins, 2001), 63.
5. Crothers, *The Man Watching*, 151.
6. Crothers, *The Man Watching*, 153.

7. Interview, February 1, 2008.

8. Longman, *The Girls of Summer*, 64.

9. Interview, February 1, 2008.

10. Crothers, *The Man Watching*, 152.

11. Crothers, *The Man Watching*, 153.

12. Crothers, *The Man Watching*, 153.

13. Karen Rosen, "Pioneers Blaze Trail to China," *Atlanta Journal-Constitution*, November 12, 1991, section E, p. 8.

14. Crothers, *The Man Watching*, 157.

15. News conference, November 17, 1991.

16. News conference, November 19, 1991.

17. News conference, November 24, 1991.

18. News conference, November 24, 1991.

19. News conference, November 24, 1991.

20. News conference, November 27, 1991.

21. News conference, November 27, 1991.

22. News conference, November 27, 1991.

23. News conference, November 27, 1991.

24. Crothers, *The Man Watching*, 158.

25. News conference, November 30, 1991.

26. Hank Hersch, "The U.S. Women's Soccer Team Is Now on Top of the World," *CNNSI.com*, December 9, 1991 (accessed February 12, 1999).

27. Hersch, "The U.S. Women's Soccer Team."

28. News conference, November 30, 1991.

29. Mia Hamm, *Go for the Goal: A Champion's Guide to Winning in Soccer and Life* (New York: HarperCollins, 1999), 208.

30. Hamm, *Go for the Goal*, 208–209.

31. Michael Lewis, "Combating a Myth from Women's World Cup '91," *CNNSI.com*, July 14, 1999 (accessed September 13, 2007).

32. Hersch, "The U.S. Women's Soccer Team."

2

Norwegian Heartbreak

Following the success of the 1991 tournament, FIFA announced that the newly christened Women's World Cup would take place in Sweden in 1995. The organizing committee decided to host the matches in small stadiums in an effort to avoid the embarrassment of empty seats. The Scandinavian nation, which had embraced the women's game long before FIFA ever decided to put together a tournament, was not the perfect setting for the U.S. to defend its title. Far from home, the Americans would have to get accustomed to the time change and different food. In addition, winning the trophy would be tougher than it was four years earlier in China. Not only were teams around the world more talented and more fit, the World Cup also doubled as a qualifier for the first-ever women's 1996 Olympic tournament (for teams that reached the quarterfinals), to be held in Atlanta. The Americans, as hosts of the Summer Games, had already qualified. For the other teams, such as hosts Sweden and favorites Norway, China, and Germany, the World Cup meant a lot more. A poor showing would mean, not only no world title, but also the chance to miss out on possible Olympic glory the following year. With two prizes on the line, the United States was in for some stiff competition.

FIFA also used the tournament as an opportunity to experiment with time-outs, which allowed a team to call a two-minute break per half. Although teams would resist using their time-outs, the rule was later restricted for use after a goal was scored or when the ball was out of bounds. Critics—fearing that such an experiment might make its way into the men's game—said that it was a ploy to squeeze in commercials during games and stifle soccer's uninterrupted flow. At the same time, FIFA extended women's games from eighty minutes to a full ninety. For once, it appeared that women's soccer had taken a step toward equality.

After the U.S victory in China in 1991, the team was essentially disbanded. With no sponsors on board and competition scarce, the team sat idle. The federation did little to promote the team (even though it was the world champion) and poured all its money and efforts into trying to make the men's team a success. Indeed, the women were overshadowed in the buildup to the male version of the World Cup finals, which the United States hosted in 1994. The men reached the round of 16, only to be bounced out of the tournament 1–0 by eventual-champion Brazil.

As for the women, players went back to their day jobs or finished up with school. It would be another four years before the United States needed to defend its title and, therefore, no hurry to bring the players together. With no sense of urgency, the program appeared to be on the brink of extinction. Dorrance, committed to the soccer program at North Carolina, resigned his post in August 1994, less than a year before the World Cup tournament; Dorrance's assistant, Tony DiCicco, was named his successor. DiCicco had been on the bench, shouting orders and rallying the players in China in 1991 as an assistant and goalkeeping coach. Now he was calling the shots. At age forty-six, DiCicco was relatively young to be a national team head coach, but he appeared to be up for the challenge.

DiCicco, however, injected an attitude that had been foreign to many men who coached women's sports: His coaching philosophy centered on the novel notion that women want to be treated like men. The women on the team wanted to be pushed and challenged just like any professional male athlete. DiCicco knew that women wanted to be pushed to succeed but, at the same time, did not want to be yelled at publicly or singled out for criticism in front of others. It was a fine line to tow, but DiCicco appeared just the person for the job.

Known for his calm demeanor, DiCicco had learned that lesson the hard way as an assistant at the 1991 tournament. Following the United States' 3–2 victory over Sweden, DiCicco had publicly criticized Lilly in front of other players following a videotape review of the game. It later got back to him that Lilly was blaming herself for the mistakes she made during the match. "Women take insults a lot more personally, so it's the job of the coach to build a relationship with his players. Build a family, in a way. Men know how to shrug it off and play on. Women really don't gain anything from having a coach get in their face," said DiCicco.[1]

If Dorrance was a stern dictator, then DiCicco's style was more democratic—although it would turn out to be no less effective in the short term. DiCicco, however, kept one mantra close to his heart, as shared by Hamm: "Coach us like men, treat us like women."[2]

When he took over the team, DiCicco still lived in his hometown of Wethersfield, Connecticut, where his home and office were less than two miles from his parents' house. He learned his love for sports from his mother, who played one-on-one basketball with him after school while he was growing up. "I never had a bias about girls playing sports. I never thought they couldn't play."[3]

DiCicco, who went on to become an All-American soccer player at Springfield College in Massachusetts, was a goalkeeper who played professionally in the American Soccer League and made only one appearance for the U.S. men's team. Although DiCicco wanted to place his own stamp on the women's team, he resisted. DiCicco was reluctant to make many personnel and lineup changes given Dorrance's past success. In retrospect, the players would complain that they had overtrained in the months leading up to the World Cup and that the mustachioed DiCicco had continued with Dorrance's blueprint for success, which centered on an arduous workout system. He may have burned out some of his players with a tough fitness regimen in the months before the tournament, but DiCicco knew that he had the talent at his disposal to repeat as world champion. Akers had a shot that resembled a canon, and Hamm possessed the skills to change the outcome of a game with the flick of a foot. DiCicco knew that both players needed to stay healthy if the Americans had any chance at attaining success. "I always give 100 percent of myself and I expect the same from my players," said DiCicco.[4]

Four years earlier, Akers was the hero in the final against Norway; in sum, she netted thirty-nine goals in twenty-six games for the team.

But in 1992, she was diagnosed with Epstein-Barr syndrome—a condition commonly referred to as chronic fatigue syndrome. Akers also went through a divorce in between World Cups (and now went just by her maiden name), but she bounced back to score twelve goals in the six months leading to the tournament and remained the team's leading scorer with eighty-two goals in eighty-eight games. Akers knew that the debilitating disease drained her energy and impeded her from playing a full game. "Oftentimes, I walk off the field, with my legs and body weighing me down like lead. My breathing is heavy and I'm often light-headed. It scares me to look in the mirror when I get like this. I shake my head knowing that I've overdone it again. I crossed that invisible line between functioning as an athlete and being very sick," said Akers (see p. 26).[5]

Hamm, however, matured over four years and slowly stepped into a leadership role. She went from precocious teen, who had just one start in 1990, to scoring sensation, replacing the "triple-edged sword" attack after Heinrichs was forced to retire because of a knee injury following the 1991 tournament.

A shy player, Hamm let her goals do the talking. She was also an unselfish player, regularly dishing off passes to teammates and running back to help the defense each time an opponent tried to create a scoring chance. DiCicco was banking on Akers and Hamm to make the difference, particularly in close games against such high-caliber opponents as China in the first round and Norway, should they meet later in the competition. DiCicco knew that Akers was questionable for an entire game given her physical limitations, but in Hamm he had a player who could go the distance.

DiCicco focused on putting together a cohesive group. If Akers and Hamm were the stars, then Carla Overbeck and Julie Foudy were the two players whom DiCicco was relying on to tell him if anyone needed to be replaced or moved to another part of the field. It was Overbeck and Foudy who alerted DiCicco to their concerns surrounding Akers's absence from practice, meetings, and weekly team dinners. "They came to me and said, 'We feel Michelle is out of the loop,'" said DiCicco.[6]

The players were aware that Akers needed to conserve her energy if she planned on playing in the World Cup, but they raised a red flag to DiCicco that they did not want her to become an outsider, jeopardizing the togetherness they had strived so hard to maintain over three years. "But on the field [Akers] still was the same

MICHELLE AKERS

Michelle Akers emerged as the first female player to gain international recognition for her playing abilities. A three-time All-American from Shorecrest High School in Shoreline, Washington, Akers went on to become a star at the National Collegiate Athletic Association level with the University of Central Florida. In college, she was a four-time All-American and was named Central Florida's Athlete of the Year following the 1988–1989 season. In 1988, she won the Hermann Trophy as the country's best female soccer player and had her no. 10 jersey retired by the school.

Photo 2.1.   Michelle Akers is inducted into the U.S. National Soccer Hall of Fame in 2004. (Credit: ISI Photos)

Akers played for the United States in the team's first-ever game, on August 18, 1985, a 1–0 loss to Italy. She scored the first goal in team history three days later against Denmark in a 2–2 tie. Akers went on to tally fifteen goals in twenty-four games for the United States from 1985 to 1990 before scoring a team record thirty-nine goals in twenty-six games in 1991 alone. Akers was also the lead scorer at the inaugural Women's World Cup in 1991, netting ten goals, including five in one game. She helped lead the team to the first world championship that year. She scored both goals in a 2–1 win over Norway.

In 1996, Akers was again a member of the U.S. team, at the Summer Olympics in Atlanta, where the team won the gold medal. In 1998, she was awarded the FIFA Order of Merit, the federation's highest honor, for her contributions to the global game of soccer. Despite having to battle chronic fatigue syndrome, Akers was again part of the U.S. team in 1999, when it captured the Women's World Cup, her second championship. Shortly before the 2000 Summer Games in Sydney, Akers retired as the United States' second-all-time leading scorer, with 105 goals.

Akers was voted FIFA's Female Player of the Century in 2002, an award she shared with China's Sun Wen. Two years later, she and Mia Hamm were the only two women named a list of the 125 greatest living soccer players, as selected by Pelé and commissioned by the sport's international governing body for its 100th anniversary. That same year, she was inducted into the U.S. National Soccer Hall of Fame.

Appearances: 153

Goals: 105

dominating player. She just couldn't go 90 minutes. It was a factor of time, how long she could play and not be wiped out for the next game," said Foudy.[7]

Even though, DiCicco was certain Akers could miss a handful of practices and withstand the rigors of the tournament. Akers's time was akin to bread during a famine; that is, DiCicco used it sparingly. Before the start of any game, Akers bargained with DiCicco over how much playing time she would get. Akers always got the upper hand, getting more minutes than DiCicco ever planned. Despite that, DiCicco was confident that Akers could overcome her condition and the enormous fatigue that came with it.

During the World Cup qualifying tournament in Montreal, Canada, Akers traveled with the team but was not expected to play much. She had limited her playing time to no more than forty minutes in previous matches. Defying logic, Akers scored six goals in four games and was named the tournament's MVP as the United States easily qualified for the World Cup. By the end of the tournament, Akers was a physical and emotional wreck. On top of that, she was divorced from her husband, Roby Stahl, a former pro soccer player whom she met in 1989. The one constant in her life was that she remained the best female player on the planet. "If she peaks, we'll peak with her," DiCicco said before the start of the World Cup.[8]

At the same time, DiCicco was not certain that Hamm had the self-confidence to be a leader. DiCicco's blueprint for success called on Hamm to not only score and create goals but be a vocal leader on and off the field. But Hamm's shyness and reluctance to speak up—once chalked up to her being young and inexperienced—was no longer an excuse. Hamm was now a veteran with a World Cup title under her belt. She was expected to be a leader. DiCicco, who understood Hamm because they had similar personalities, was relying on her to be his eyes and ears on the field during games.

In April 1995, just two months before the start of the World Cup, DiCicco and Hamm got into a heated argument on the field during an exhibition game against Italy in Poissy, France. Hamm's criticism of how he was coaching the team, particularly how DiCicco was hounding midfielder Tiffeny Roberts, triggered a verbal spat. DiCicco thought Hamm was out of line and disrespectful. "Worry about your own game, it needs work," DiCicco barked back.[9]

At halftime, a visibly distraught Hamm kicked a door as she entered the locker room. DiCicco was also upset and prepared to bench Hamm until Overbeck stepped in to restore calm. The next day, DiCicco admitted to Hamm that he had been overcoaching Roberts.[10] Hamm also apologized for yelling at him. DiCicco said that when he told Hamm that her observation was "probably right," he showed her how vulnerable he could be.[11] "I apologized to [Hamm] in front of the team and they told me they respected me even more after that," recalled DiCicco.[12] It worked. Later the same day, Hamm scored a hat trick as the Americans defeated Canada 5–0.

Since they had no domestic league, the Americans set up camp in Florida, full-time, almost two years before the World Cup; as such, they entered the tournament as favorites. DiCicco knew that before he and his players could open any champagne, they had to defeat the world's best teams. In February, the World Cup draw yielded a treacherous first-round group: The Americans were paired with China, Denmark, and Australia. The possibility of securing wins against Denmark and Australia appeared likely, although the game against China was expected to be the toughest.

DiCicco's team—physically fitter than any of the other teams at the tournament—played its first game on June 7 in the town of Galve against China. The match turned out to be even tougher for the Americans than they first expected. The United States—featuring three defenders, with the five-player midfield pushing forward to take advantage of the counterattack—appeared in control of the game from the start, taking the lead after twenty-two minutes with Tisha Venturini, a UNC graduate who made her national team debut in 1992. DiCicco's team doubled its lead in the thirty-fifth minute with Tiffeny Milbrett on a rebound off Lilly's twenty-yard free kick. "I happened to be at the right place at the right time. It was an easy goal," she said.[13]

Milbrett, who graduated from the University of Portland on the eve of the tournament, came into the game after eighteen minutes when Akers sustained a concussion and a banged-up right knee in the sixth minute, after bumping heads with a Chinese defender who was trying to clear the ball following a corner kick. As Akers left the field unconscious, DiCicco made the decision to replace her with Milbrett, a member of the U.S. Under-20 team since 1990. "You always want to come in with a bang and I guess I came in and made a statement," Milbrett said.[14]

The Americans did appear to be in control and with a 2–0 lead, a victory appeared a real possibility. But the never-say-die Chinese picked up the tempo, using crisp passing to move the ball into the American half. China's efforts were rewarded with a goal by Liping Wang in the thirty-eighth minute. The United States, a bit battered and bruised, went into halftime with a slim 2–1 lead.

The second half featured more fireworks and a U.S. meltdown. Hamm scored again for the United States in the fifty-first minute. The goal made DiCicco more comfortable as he barked orders from the sidelines, but he was still distressed at the defense's inability to always clear balls. DiCicco's orders fell on deaf ears. The

Americans—although comfortably ahead 3–1—were in for a surprise. The Chinese answered back with two goals in a five-minute span to tie the game. Sun Wen, China's most prolific striker, tied the match in the seventy-ninth minute at 3–3 after she unleashed a laser beam of a shot from inside the penalty area that beat goalkeeper Briana Scurry. "I thought China played a very good game and deserved to tie," said DiCicco.[15]

DiCicco's biggest worry after the game was not so much his team's second-half breakdown, but whether Akers would be fit to play in the next game, which was scheduled two days later against Denmark. The Danes had posted a 5–0 win over Australia and appeared to be a formidable opponent for the Americans. Akers had bounced back from chronic fatigue syndrome before, but her injuries appeared to have won out this time. Akers's concussion and knee injury were worse than she expected, and team doctors recommended that she sit out the Denmark game. DiCicco agreed.

On June 9, the United States took to the field, once again in Gavle, against Denmark. DiCicco went with Milbrett in place of Akers, who watched the game from the stands. The Americans got on the board first when Lilly put the ball in the net off a header after just eight minutes. The United States put the game away in the second half when Milbrett—off a perfect pass from Hamm—tallied her second goal in as many games in the forty-ninth minute, putting through a low but powerful shot past Danish goalkeeper Dorthe Larsen. "I actually [was aiming for] the far post and it went near," said Milbrett.[16]

The United States could have won by a much larger margin, but it squandered six scoring chances, mostly because DiCicco implemented a possession-style offense meant to thwart any effort of a Danish comeback, as China successfully did late in the previous game. Under that system, the U.S. strikers often held the ball too long, squandering scoring chances in the process. But the tactic was useful in other ways, running time off the clock and forcing opposing defenders to spend a lot of energy trying to chase around Hamm and her teammates. "We played with lots of high pressure and oftentimes we burned ourselves out. That's why we've always had to be in better shape than our opponents, just so we can keep up with ourselves," Hamm joked.[17]

The only odd footnote to the game was Scurry's ejection with two minutes left to play. The controversial decision by referee Mamadouba Camara of Guinea came when he saw Scurry step too far out of the penalty box with the ball as she went to punt it. It was a routine play, one Scurry and other goalkeepers had done countless times before. When Scurry put one foot over the line, Camara's assistant lifted his flag. Camara ran over and pulled out a red card. The ejection, which carried with it a two-game suspension, infuriated DiCicco. "In the spirit of the game, that was an incorrect call," he said.[18]

Heinrichs, DiCicco's assistant and a veteran of the team that won the tournament in 1991, called Hamm over to the sidelines. Heinrichs casually put her arm around her and said, "Mia, we've used all our substitutes, and we're going to put you in goal. How do you feel about that?"[19] Hamm did not know how to feel. She was numb for about a second. Then, Hamm shot back, "Why don't you use a real goalkeeper?"[20] "We've used all our subs," Heinrichs replied.[21] Then it hit Hamm: Not only did she have to play goal, but Denmark had a free kick from about twenty yards out as a result of Scurry's handling the ball.

DiCicco, who was out of substitutions after having made all three allotted to a team, put Hamm in net. She was stunned. Nonetheless, she put on the gloves and slowly took her place between the posts. "Until that time, my only goalkeeping experience had been limited to some end-of-practice crossing drills where my teammates took great delight in nailing me with the ball, but I guess I saved a few, because the coaches decided that it was I who should step between the pipes."[22]

On the ensuing Danish free kick, defender Kamma Flaeng kicked the ball high. Hamm, who appeared uncomfortable and too withdrawn from the wall of U.S. players, watched with relief as the ball sailed high over the crossbar. "I like to think I would have saved it . . . but of course, we'll never know!" recalled Hamm.[23]

She only wound up touching the ball twice, one of them counting as a save off a clumsily kicked ball. When the final whistle blew, a look of relief crossed DiCicco's face. Overbeck ran over to Hamm after the game, summing up how the entire team felt about seeing her finish the game in goal. "You know Mia, I was pretty confident with you going back there—I mean you're a good athlete—until I turned around and you looked about the size of a peanut in goal," Overbeck said.[24]

After the game, DiCicco announced that the United States had filed a formal protest against the decision to eject Scurry. Danish officials said they would support the United States. In the end, FIFA handed Scurry a one-game ban. As for the outcome of the Denmark game, the 2–0 victory boded well and kept the team's hopes of reaching the elimination round very much alive. "We're really pleased with the result. We played hard," said DiCicco.[25]

The United States' next hurdle was Australia. With one game left in the first round, the United States and China were tied for first place in the group with four points each, although the Chinese had an edge because they had scored more goals than the Americans. For the United States to finish first, it had to not only defeat Australia but score more goals than China could muster in its final group game against Denmark.

Both games kicked off at the same time on June 10. The Americans took on the Aussies at Olympia Stadium in Helsingborg at 4:00 PM. DiCicco knew that he would have to spend the afternoon focused on his game but also do a fair amount of scoreboard watching. The United States wanted to avoid finishing second—and run the risk of playing the Swedes in the next round—and, instead, focused on finishing first and being matched up with a weaker opponent. "We felt sure we could put more than a couple of goals in the back of the net," said Hamm.[26]

She was not so sure, however, after the first half ended scoreless. The Americans had dominated, but it did not result in a goal. The closest that the United States had come was when Venturini's shot slammed off the crossbar five minutes into the game. Meanwhile, in the other game, China and Denmark were deadlocked 1–1 at halftime. If the scores remained the same, China would win the group. The United States would finish second.

After a DiCicco pep talk at halftime, the Americans—still missing Akers because of injury—were confident that they could score a few goals and put the game away. Milbrett, who had scored two so far, unleashed a shot from long range that goalkeeper Tracey Wheeler could not get to. The ball had other plans, however, and hit the post for a second time that afternoon. Australia, which had no chance of advancing to the next round, also had other plans. The Aussies' defense-minded tactics kept the Americans off the board but allowed them to maneuver the ball forward every so often and attempt to score on the counterattack. In the fifty-fourth minute, the Aussies put together their first real scoring attempt. Midfielder Angela Iannotta's cross found an unmarked seventeen-year-old Lisa

Casagrande. The teen headed the ball into the net past backup goal-keeper Saskia Webber for the 1–0 lead.

The Americans were stunned but forced to react. The goal brought to life what had been a relatively boring game and also appeared to energize the Americans. Eight minutes after Casagrande's goal, Hamm forced a corner kick following a dazzling solo run, dribbling past three defenders, only to see the ball go out of bounds. Hamm took the corner and Foudy, who came off the bench just three minutes earlier for striker Amanda Cromwell, headed the ball past Wheeler to tie the score. Joy Fawcett made it 2–1 in the seventy-first minute, knocking in a rebound from close range after Wheeler had tried to save a shot from Lilly. Meanwhile, the U.S. bench was keeping close tabs on the China–Denmark game thanks to a phone.

As the Americans celebrated Fawcett's goal, the phone rang: China was up 2–1. With two minutes left to play, Hamm was tripped in the penalty box. Overbeck converted the ensuing penalty kick, drilling the ball past Wheeler to make it 3–1 two minutes into stoppage time. DiCicco could finally breathe a sigh of relief. The Americans had scored one more goal than China. Or so he thought. As the team celebrated, the phone rang again: China scored in the final minute to go up 3–1. The players on the bench were frantic. DiCicco calmly got their attention, shouting, "One more! Gotta have one more!"[27]

In the ninety-fourth minute—a full four minutes into stoppage time—the United States did the unthinkable. As a chilly wind swept across the field, Hamm played the ball past a few Aussie defenders, dishing off a pass that found Debbie Keller, who slotted the ball past Wheeler. Keller, a former North Carolina standout and a Hermann Trophy finalist the previous year, celebrated with her teammates. The United States won 4–1, and the last-gasp goal won them the group. China defeated Denmark 3–1, and the Americans scored that one extra goal that appeared to elude them for much of the contest. "They're an amazing group. They went out and got another goal," DiCicco said.[28]

Hamm, who was involved in all four goals, sported an ear-to-ear grin as she walked of the field. "We scored four goals in the second half against Australia, every one crucial, and we did this because every player truly believed we could and took action to make it happen. That was mental toughness," she said.[29]

The quarterfinals were set. The United States would play Japan, with the winner facing the victor of Norway versus Denmark. On the other side of the bracket, host Sweden was matched with China, whereas Germany was pitted against up-and-comer England.

Hamm knew that the team's mental toughness had to continue into the elimination round if it had any hope of winning the tournament. From this point on, every game was do-or-die. In many ways, the tournament was just getting started. Scurry would be back in goal for the quarterfinals, but Akers's health was still a huge question mark. "I've been running and doing a little ball work. . . . My knee is extremely sore and I have a slight headache, but I know I'll be ready," said Akers.[30]

Against Japan, Akers was in uniform and on the bench as she watched her teammates take the field on June 13 in Gavle. Milbrett again filled the void left by Akers up top, with Hamm, Lilly, and Venturini expected to churn out plays from the midfield. In the end, Japan was no match for the Americans. Lilly put the United States ahead after eight minutes and added another in the forty-second. Milbrett tallied another three minutes later to put the United States ahead 3–0 at halftime. With the Americans comfortably ahead, DiCicco opted to give Akers more time to recover and smartly kept her on the sidelines. Also, he took out Hamm and Lilly to give them more time to rest in lieu of the semifinals. Even without Hamm and Lilly, the United States overpowered the Japanese defense and scored once again with Venturini ten minutes from time to make it 4–0.

DiCicco's team landed in the semifinals. Two more wins to the title. Repeating as world champions appeared a real possibility. With Akers healthy again and Hamm and Lilly playing at their full potential, the Americans appeared unstoppable. The victory over Japan boosted their confidence going into the game against Norway.

The U.S.–Norway game was expected to be a competitive affair. It was a rematch of the 1991 championship game, and Norway was looking for revenge. The Norwegians—traditionally one of the best teams in the world until the Americans knocked them off their pedestal—were hungry for victory. Anything short of winning the World Cup would be a disappointment.

The Americans, however, knew not to underestimate their Scandinavian opponents. Norway was fundamentally the best team at the tournament. They were precise on set pieces, which worried Scurry and the U.S. defense. Defensively, Norway was good at maintaining possession and clearing balls. DiCicco knew that Norway would use those tools against them. Just how well they would be able to execute those plays against the United States was anyone's guess.

The United States and Norway squared off in Vasteras on June 15 at Arosvallen Stadium. DiCicco benched Milbrett in favor of Akers and paired her with Hamm and Foudy in the midfield. Offensively, Lilly and Venturini were given the task of helping put the Americans on the board. Norway featured six-foot striker Ann Kristin Aarones, a one-woman scoring machine and one of the best players on the planet. It was the U.S. defense's responsibility to make sure that she did not get free in the box. Failure to contain her, DiCicco knew, could result in a Norway goal.

Aarones had scored five goals during the tournament, two of them off headers, given her height advantage over most defenders. The Norwegians wasted no time trying to score. In the tenth minute, Aarones headed the ball just under the crossbar and past Scurry to put Norway up 1–0. The goal had predictably come off an in-swinging corner kick that defender Gro Espeseth floated for Aarones's head. "I know Briana went for it, but she didn't get a touch to it," observed DiCicco.[31]

The United States was slow to react. Even more sluggish was Akers, who was playing her first game since the tournament opener. As Akers played the ball, Norwegian defenders took every chance to rough her up. Although she had made her way back into the lineup, Akers was too banged up to do anything. "Michelle wasn't quite 100 percent. She didn't have her burst of speed. It's a shame for her because she worked so hard to get back into this world championship," DiCicco noted.[32]

The Americans labored on, even without Akers at 100 percent. Hamm and Foudy tried to fill that void, but Espeseth and the Norwegian defense did not let up, using their physical game, highlighted by rough tackles, to stifle the U.S. offense. The first half ended with the United States down 1–0. The second half was more of the same. DiCicco kept Akers in the game, hoping that she could muster the energy to create a play or two. It never happened.

The situation finally opened up for the United States in the seventy-sixth minute after Norway captain Heidi Store received a second yellow card and was ejected. Down a player, Norway was not so adventurous offensively. The Americans benefited from the player advantage and began to apply pressure on the Norwegian defense. The United States needed the late-game heroics reminiscent of their first-round victory over Australia. Defender Joy Fawcett could have been the hero, but her two scoring attempts hit the crossbar in the last five minutes of the match. In the end, Norway won the game, 1–0, and exacted revenge on the Americans. "They dominated the first 35 minutes of the game in classic Norway style. We couldn't get a grasp of the game and during that time the game was won. After that we clawed our way back in. I was extremely proud of the way our players fought in the second half," said DiCicco.[33]

For Norway, it was their fourth shutout in five tournament games. The United States may have been outplayed in the first half, but upping the tempo in the final twenty minutes could have easily resulted in a goal. Hitting the crossbar twice was another indication that it was not the United States' day. "I'm going to measure that goal to make sure it's eight feet tall," DiCicco joked after the game.[34]

It was the first game at the tournament where the Americans failed to score, although the Norwegians were not so sure they could win the game until the end. "The game was a lot tougher than I expected. We weren't sure we were going to win until the referee blew the whistle," said Aarones.[35]

DiCicco's only regret may have been going with Akers, but even that might not have been enough to defeat Norway. "In a tight game like this, I still wanted Michelle in at the end of the game," said DiCicco.[36]

Hamm, who until this point had been one of the tournament's best players, said that they had allowed the Norwegians to "dictate the game, hoping that they would make mistakes and leave the door open."[37] Hamm also blamed the loss on herself and her teammates' lack of determination against such a high-profile opponent. "On that day they were clearly the better team. They were mentally tough and we weren't," she said.[38]

While the Americans wallowed in their anguish, the Norwegians flaunted their win. The players got on their hands and knees and formed a worm-like conga line, crawling around the field in celebration as Hamm, Akers, and the rest of the team watched in disgust. It appeared to be a harmless celebration to Norway fans, but it was one that broke the U.S. players' hearts. For DiCicco's players, the loss was a humiliation, and the Norwegians were being bad sports, using a childish celebration to rub it in. "It was easily the longest 10 minutes of my soccer life, and I can assure you I haven't forgotten it because none of us looked away," recalled Hamm.[39] Some of the U.S. players cried, their eyes swelling up as the Norwegians laughed.

"We swore we'd never feel that way again and that the next time we met, it would be us in a pile of happy, sweaty bodies at the final whistle," said Hamm.[40]

Even Norway's coach, Evan Pellerud, had nothing nice to say about the Americans after the game. "I was disappointed by the Americans. They were stronger four years ago, especially offensively," he said.[41]

All that was left for the United States was the formality of playing for third place. The Americans played China on June 17 in Gavle, a rematch of their thrilling 3–3 first-round game. A goal in each half—one by Venturini in the twenty-fourth minute and Hamm in the fifty-fifth—gave the Americans a 2–0 win. Fittingly, it was Hamm who led the team to a place on the podium. Venturini's goal, a header that slipped past Chinese goalkeeper Hong Gao, was her third at the tournament, tying her for the team lead with Milbrett and Lilly.

Hamm's goal was one of the greatest individual performances at the tournament. She picked up a loose ball deep in midfield, outran a Chinese defender, and then fired a low ball once she got into the penalty box, beating Gao's outstretched arms. The goal would have made Hamm's childhood idol, Argentine soccer star Diego Maradona, proud.

Akers, meanwhile, sat on the bench and nursed her banged-up body as Milbrett got the start. Akers watched as her teammates won the game, bouncing back from the devastating loss to Norway just two days earlier. Although the victory over China was sweet, the third-place finish was no remedy for the previous loss, which was still fresh on their minds. "We'll be all right. . . . As far as I'm concerned, the Olympics are more important. I think we're going to be ready. It's a year away. We'll get over this," said Scurry.[42]

Norway, meanwhile, went on to win the World Cup, posting a 2–0 win over Germany and heading to the 1996 Atlanta Games as favorites to win the gold medal. As for the Americans, the players wanted revenge. The battle for gold had begun.

NOTES

1. Interview, June 19, 1999.
2. Interview, June 19, 1999.
3. Jere Longman, *The Girls of Summer: The U.S. Women's Soccer Team and How It Changed the World* (New York: HarperCollins, 2001), 170.

4. Interview, June 19, 1999.

5. Interview, June 19, 1999.

6. Longman, *The Girls of Summer*, 171.

7. Kelly Whiteside, "Michelle Akers Is Ready to Lead the U.S. to Another Title," *CNNSI.com*, June 5, 1995 (accessed February 12, 1999).

8. Whiteside, "Michelle Akers Is Ready."

9. Longman, *The Girls of Summer*, 171.

10. Longman, *The Girls of Summer*, 171.

11. Longman, *The Girls of Summer*, 172.

12. Longman, *The Girls of Summer*, 172.

13. Stephan Nasstrom, "U.S. 3, China 3," Associated Press, June 7, 1995.

14. Nasstrom, "U.S. 3, China 3."

15. Nasstrom, "U.S. 3, China 3."

16. Stephan Nasstrom, "U.S. 2, Denmark 0," Associated Press, June 9, 1995.

17. Interview, June 19, 1999.

18. Nasstrom, "U.S. 2, Denmark 0."

19. Mia Hamm, *Go for the Goal: A Champion's Guide to Winning in Soccer and Life* (New York: HarperCollins, 1999), 180.

20. Hamm, *Go for the Goal*, 180.

21. Hamm, *Go for the Goal*, 180.

22. Hamm, *Go for the Goal*, 178.

23. Hamm, *Go for the Goal*, 181.

24. Hamm, *Go for the Goal*, 182.

25. Nasstrom, "U.S. 2, Denmark 0."

26. Hamm, *Go for the Goal*, 34.

27. Hamm, *Go for the Goal*, 35.

28. News conference, June 10, 1995.

29. Hamm, *Go for the Goal*, 35.

30. Stephan Nasstrom, "U.S. 4, Australia 1," Associated Press, June 10, 1995.

31. Stephan Nasstrom, "Norway 1, U.S. 0," Associated Press, June 16, 1995.

32. Nasstrom, "Norway 1, U.S. 0."

33. Nasstrom, "Norway 1, U.S. 0."

34. News conference, June 15, 1995.

35. News conference, June 15, 1995.

36. News conference, June 15, 1995.

37. Hamm, *Go for the Goal*, 46.

38. Hamm, *Go for the Goal*, 46.

39. Hamm, *Go for the Goal*, 97.

40. Hamm, *Go for the Goal*, 197–198.

41. News conference, June 15, 1995.

42. Stephan Nasstrom, "U.S. 2, China 0," Associated Press, June 17, 1995.

3

The Golden Girls

R evenge.
That was on the minds of DiCicco and his players as they prepared for the Atlanta Games. Women's soccer had never been an Olympic event, and the United States wanted to make sure that it would be the first to capture gold. DiCicco's hopes of guiding his players to the top of the podium hit a major snag when nine failed to report to training camp on December 5, some eight months before the Olympics, because of a contract dispute with the federation. The strike ended a month later in early 1996, but failure to report back to work at their full-time training center in Florida put all parties on edge for weeks.

Although U.S. Soccer executive director Hank Steinbrecher expressed hurt and disappointment at the work stoppage, the players' lawyer, Ellen Zavian, claimed there was no bitterness between the players and U.S. Soccer. It was simply a matter of negotiation. "To my knowledge, it was the first time professional sportswomen didn't sign a contract with a federation. The [U.S.] federation was quite surprised, I think, but these women showed a lot of chutzpah—more than any man I've represented—by standing up for what they believe in," said Zavian, a Baltimore-based lawyer who had also represented National Football League players.[1]

The main sticking point was the federation's offer of a $250,000 team bonus for winning the gold medal—and nothing for any other finish. Zavian said the deal offered by U.S. Soccer showed that a "silver and bronze medal was mediocrity. . . . You can see why that sort of thinking was simply appalling to [the players]."[2] Eventually, both sides settled for a $240,000 gold medal bonus and $115,000 for a silver. Zavian also brokered individual bonuses for the sixteen players named to the final roster that June.

It was the Olympics that kept many of the players in the sport for so long. Certainly, Overbeck and the seven others—Hamm, Akers, Lilly, Fawcett, Foudy, Venturini, and Scurry—formed the team's core. Without them, there really was no team. "I love the game and I'd play for free if I had to. But we've been on this team for a long time and we deserved certain things," said Fawcett.[3]

The voluminous Foudy, who had become a more vocal presence on the field and in the locker room, took it upon herself to get the word out that the team was being disrespected. She talked sportswriters' ears off about the ongoing labor dispute and, in the process, earned the nickname "Loudy Foudy" from her teammates. Her quick wit and refreshing candor instantly made her a team leader and a media darling. "This was something that was very, very important to us. We were not going to back down. We had come so far. Without us, there was no team," proclaimed Foudy.[4]

The federation needed the players almost more than the players needed the team. Eventually, U.S. Soccer caved, and the team's Olympic gold medal hopes remained alive. "I think this whole thing has shown that the [U.S.] women's team has come a long, long way in the last few years," said Venturini.[5]

A year before the walkout, the federation housed the women's team at a state-of-the-art training center in Sanford, Florida, with the players earning as much as $4,000 a month—more than any of the U.S. national team's male players during their preparations for the 1994 World Cup. During their training for the Olympic Games, the federation budgeted $1.6 million on the women's team—three times more than the men's team.[6]

With the contract dispute finally behind them, the women could focus on preparing for Atlanta. The Americans and reigning world champion Norway were favorites to reach the final. The Olympic draw even made it such that if each team won its respective round-robin group—a distinct possibility—then both sides could square off only in the final.

The United States was placed in the first-round, round-robin group alongside rivals China, Sweden, and Denmark. Not an easy group, but the Americans vowed to win—against anyone. "We are capable of beating anyone in the world," DiCicco often told his players to pump them up before a game.[7]

The rally cry was in fact much more than just plain talk. The Americans entered the Olympics in July 1996 with an impressive 17–1–1 record. Norway had officially been put on alert. The Norwegians, meanwhile, were grouped with up-and-comers Brazil, Germany, and Japan. Also not an easy grouping, but Norway was far and away the best team.

Although the Olympics were being held in Atlanta, the men's and women's soccer tournaments would be played at a variety of venues scattered across the South, including Orlando and Miami, Florida; Birmingham, Alabama; and Washington, D.C. Only the semifinals and gold and bronze medal matches were to be played in Athens, in suburban Atlanta.

On July 21, the United States made its Olympic debut against Denmark. All indications pointed to a U.S. victory, and the twenty-five thousand screaming fans that showed up at the Citrus Bowl in Orlando were banking on it. Thousands of screaming girls—many with their faces painted red, white, and blue—chanted "USA! USA!" incessantly throughout much of the game and reserved their loudest shrieks for Hamm. The stifling Florida heat turned the stadium into a steamy cauldron—one the Danes were not used to—and the Americans took full advantage of their Florida training. When told after the game of the 102-degree temperature that day, DiCicco smiled and responded, "Perfect."[8]

The United States controlled the pace from the start and scored in the thirty-sixth minute with Venturini, who turned a throw-in from Brandi Chastain into a goal. After latching onto the ball, Venturini unleashed a shot that banked off the post and into the net past Danish goalkeeper Dorthe Larsen. Ten minutes later, Hamm, spurred on by the crowd, took a pass from Akers, sprinted ten yards and blasted a powerful shot of her own that found its way into the left corner past Larsen. The flag-waving crowd—the largest in the nation to ever see a U.S. women's soccer game—jumped to its feet and applauded. "The crowd was absolutely unbelievable," Hamm said.[9]

With a 2–0 lead at halftime, the Americans maintained their offensive pressure on the Danes. Milbrett scored in the forty-ninth minute on a pass from Hamm. The goal sealed a 3–0 win and put the Americans in first place along with China, which grabbed a 2–0 victory over Sweden later that day.

Despite the three goals and outshooting the Danes 22–0, the U.S. players were more impressed with the fans than with themselves. "It was electric," gushed Hamm. "Unbelievable!"[10] Overbeck was also amazed: "I got goose bumps walking onto the field. . . . You know, that's never happened to me before," she said.[11]

Two days later, DiCicco was hoping for a repeat performance in steamy Orlando. Sweden was not the toughest team on the planet, but it was expected to put on a better showing than its northern European sisters. On the plus side, the Swedes were skillful, aggressive, and physical. On the negative, they were not used to playing in such warm conditions.

Both sides came out looking for a goal almost from the start as twenty-eight thousand fans filed into the Citrus Bowl. In the first minute, Venturini knocked a header that slammed off the crossbar. Less than a minute later, a loose ball in the U.S. penalty area was shot wide of the goal guarded by Scurry (see next page). The Swedes did not stop there. Scurry thwarted two more attempts as the U.S. defense tried to stop the onslaught of Swedish scoring attempts. In the fourteenth minute, Venturini headed the ball past goalkeeper Annelie Nilsson off a Milbrett pass to take a 1–0 lead. DiCicco's squad turned up the pressure and nearly scored in the twenty-second minute when a Foudy free kick from twenty yards skimmed the post. With seconds left in the first half, Venturini failed to score once again; this time, her shot deflected off Nilsson and off the post.

In the second half, the attack-minded Swedes, in need of a win if they had any hope of advancing to the semifinals, tried in vain to get by the tenacious U.S. defense. DiCicco—confident that Foudy and Lilly were all they needed to stop the Swedish game at midfield—moved Shannon MacMillan into the forward position, alongside Hamm and Akers, for a three-pronged attack. The move paid off within two minutes when MacMillan buried the ball into the back of the net in the sixty-third minute to make it 2–0. Not to be outdone, Sweden pulled one back two minutes later when a free kick deflected off Overbeck's knee for the 2–1 final score.

Such a physical contest had left the American players bruised. With nine minutes left to play, Hamm sprained her left ankle fol-

BRIANA SCURRY

Briana Scurry will always be remembered as one of the U.S. team's greatest goalkeepers. A mainstay between the pipes, Scurry started in net for the United States at five major competitions, including the 1995 World Cup, the 1996 Olympics, the 1999 World Cup, the 2003 World Cup, and the 2004 Olympics.

Scurry was an All-American at Anoka Senior High School in Anoka, Minnesota. Named a second-team All-American in 1993, she helped lead the University of Massachusetts to a 17–3–3 record and the semifinals at the National Collegiate Athletic Association tournament. Scurry went on to complete her college career with thirty-seven

Photo 3.1.   Briana Scurry takes a break during practice. (Credit: ISI Photos)

shutouts in sixty-five starts with an outstanding 48–13–4 record and an equally stunning 0.56 goals against average. In 1992, she also played three games as a forward despite her wonderful goalkeeping abilities.

Her abilities caught the eye of U.S. coach Tony DiCicco in 1994 and a year later she got the starting nod at the World Cup. At the 1996 Olympics, she played in every minute of all five of the United States' games and conceded just three goals. Scurry promised her teammates that she would run naked through the streets if the team won gold—a promise she made good on when she streaked through a desolate neighborhood in Athens, Georgia.

Scurry was also vital when the United States won the 1999 World Cup and was in net when the Americans defeated China on penalty kicks in the final. The gold-medal triumph at the 2004 Athens Games was the last one for the United States featuring Scurry as a starter. At the 2000 Olympics, Scurry was named the team's second goalkeeper after Siri Mullinix was given the start. Scurry struggled to get playing time after 2004 and was once again demoted to the bench when she was named as a backup to Hope Solo at the 2007 World Cup. Scurry, who had been riding the bench the whole tournament, was given the start in the semifinals against Brazil by coach Greg Ryan. An embarrassing 4–0 loss prompted Solo to lash out against Scurry during a postgame interview. Scurry and Solo later reconciled. Scurry was not chosen by coach Pia Sundhage for the U.S. Olympic team that eventually won gold at the 2008 Beijing Games.

With 173 caps, Scurry, who is no longer in the U.S. player pool, is the goalkeeper with the most appearances for the team.

Appearances: 173
Goals: 0

lowing a collision with Nilsson. She was taken out in the eighty-fifth minute and replaced with Gabarra. X-rays later revealed no fracture, and DiCicco announced after the game that she would probably sit out the China game to stay fresh for the medal round. "She's resting comfortably, but doctors are taking every precaution," DiCicco explained as reporters peppered him with questions after the game.[12]

The Americans had clinched a semifinal berth along with China, who also remained undefeated. Although the U.S.–China game had no bearing on who would advance, first place in the group—and a chance to avoid Norway in the semifinals—was still on the line. China had a slight edge, having scored two more goals than the Americans following a 5–1 trouncing of Denmark. The Norwegians had followed the script. Following a 4–0 rout of Japan, Norway clinched a semifinal berth. Now it found itself on a collision course with the Americans.

On July 25, the United States and China squared off at the Orange Bowl in Miami, Florida. More than forty-three thousand fans—a U.S. record for fans at a women's soccer game—jammed into the stadium to watch Hamm and her teammates in what was increasingly becoming one of the most popular tickets at the Olympics, alongside men's basketball and women's gymnastics.

Hamm could only watch from the sidelines as the United States and China played to a scoreless draw. Hamm, who was still nursing a sprained ankle, sat on the bench. At times, she used her clipboard to help the coaching staff make tactical moves. The fans, disappointed not to see her play, were delighted when she strolled around the field as her teammates practiced drills and took turns kicking balls at Scurry before the start of the game. Afterward, the question on everyone's mind was whether Hamm's absence had been the reason for the lack of scoring. "It's hard to say. Certainly, she's a force when she's out there," admitted DiCicco.[13]

The tie ended the United States' fifteen-game winning streak and marked the first time that year that the Americans had been held scoreless. The game itself was no more exciting than a training session. Chinese speed versus American strength produced a dull match. With nothing at stake—because both teams had made the medal round—the game became nothing more than a formality. Although the game featured methodical play by both teams, the United States could have actually won with three minutes left to play: Off a corner kick, both Overbeck and Cindy Parlow tried to head the ball. Chastain attempted a shot that was thwarted. Parlow then missed a clear chance on the ensuing corner kick.

The tie, however, had negative consequences. It ensured that the United States would finish second in the group because of goal differential and therefore play Norway in the semifinals. China would face Brazil in the other semifinal. "We really wanted to win our group [in order to avoid Norway]. We really didn't get what we wanted," DiCicco said.[14]

DiCicco knew that Hamm needed to be healthy, and the rest of the roster needed to step up, if the United States wanted to play for the gold and exact revenge on Norway. "We are capable of beating anyone in the world," DiCicco boldly proclaimed on the eve of the game.[15]

The statement was not just merely a prediction but part of a winning attitude that DiCicco tried to instill in his team and coaching staff since the World Cup elimination a year earlier. Both the United States and Norway had hogged the spotlight in women's soccer for the past decade. Now the world's two biggest women's soccer powers were preparing to meet again. The two teams had put together some classic performances in the past. With a shot at playing for gold, both sides were expected to put in their best efforts.

At this point in the competition, the United States' success was largely credited to DiCicco's tactics and coaching methods along with Hamm's well-timed runs and goals. The person whom they needed to thank most, however, was team psychologist Colleen Hacker, who held a doctorate from the University of Oregon and once coached women's soccer at Pacific Lutheran University for 17 seasons.

After losing to Norway, DiCicco took the unprecedented step of hiring a sports psychologist. He wanted his team to have a mental edge over his opponents. A series of drills that Hacker devised were meant to inspire and mentally prepare the players for such arduous competition. One of those exercises involved sprinting up the steep concrete steps of a building on the University of Georgia's campus as the players enthusiastically belted out the theme from the classic movie *Rocky*. Silly? Maybe. Effective? Absolutely.

Another exercise—conducted before the start of the Olympic tournament—involved driving the players to the top of a cliff in Portland, Oregon. Once there, half the players were blindfolded and then led by their teammates down a steep ledge, only a few feet wide in places, as a way of gaining trust and confidence. The drill, a staple among higher-ups in corporate jobs, had never really been attempted by athletes. Although the exercises appeared odd to some of the players, DiCicco widely credited Hacker's unusual methods with bolstering his players' confidence and concentration while building a bond among them and fostering team chemistry.

DiCicco gave Hacker the title of "mental skills coach" when he pleaded with the federation to set aside the funds to hire her full-time. A grant from the U.S. Olympic Committee funded Hacker's early work with the team, and a full-time position soon followed after U.S. Soccer was convinced that she could help instill a winning attitude in the team. "I made fun of it. Team bonding, when I played, was running. If I had a mental problem, I ran. I'm from the old school, but I fully appreciate it's a new day and new age in contemporary sport," said Steinbrecher.[16]

The players quickly accepted Hacker. After all, three players on the team, including Overbeck, had degrees in psychology. Akers's father was a psychologist, and assistant coach Lauren Gregg had a master's degree in consulting psychology. "I've never seen anyone come in and be accepted so fast by the team," Milbrett recalled.[17]

Following the loss to Norway, players blamed it on a bevy of factors: A failure to eliminate distractions, an injury to Akers in their first game, an ongoing dispute with the federation over what brand of shoes they could wear, and the presence of family at the games (and a ticket allotment feud) all compounded to the problem.

To deal with these issues and any others that may have sprung up during preparation for the Olympics, Hacker appointed two parents—Chastain's and Overbeck's mothers—as "captains" of the team's traveling and ever-growing group of friends and families. Lark Chastain and Sandra Werden were told to act as intermediaries between players' loved ones and the federation. Hacker also gave the players audiotapes that they had to listen to before the start of a game. The tapes included personalized positive messages meant to motivate them.

But what seemed to be psychobabble to most reporters and soccer pundits was working wonders. The United States was in the semifinals, and the players were as ready as they would ever be to take on such a tough opponent. "These players do not view anything other than triumph as an option. Losing is not contemplated, it is not addressed, it is not one of the options," said Hacker.[18]

As the Americans continued to advance, their confidence grew by leaps and bounds, but such confidence largely rested on Hamm's shoulders, despite any talk of team unity. She was hands down the star of the tournament, and the best female soccer player on the planet. As the Olympics had proven until this point, Hamm was without peer in her position. She was comfortable not only running with the ball but also assuming the added responsibility of scoring goals for the team. More than that, Hamm helped shaped the outcome of games, directing them like Martin Scorcese would a movie. She ordered events to happen according to her infinite imagination and will. Her majestic passes and powerful shots conveyed a precision never before seen in a female player. Her ability to read the game was without precedent for a female soccer player. Hamm was also an astute athlete, playing with her mind and her feet; against Norway, Hamm and her teammates would need both. Above all, they would need heart to win.

The United States and Norway faced off on July 28 at Sanford Stadium in Athens. One of the world's best female referees, Sonia Denoncourt of Canada, was given the responsibility of overseeing the clash. More than sixty-four thousand fans packed the stands, waving American flags and chanting "USA! USA!" from the opening whistle. The turnout had been a shock to organizers and the International Olympic Committee, who only four years earlier had not even planned to include women's soccer at the Games. Blinding camera flashes flickered from all parts of the packed stadium, and the awestruck Americans were prepared to do battle against the world champions.

The United States got off to a poor start as Medalen put Norway ahead after only eighteen minutes. The Americans controlled the pace and possession for large chunks of the game from that moment on, moving the ball across the field for much of the contest in a bid to grab back a goal.

Just when the Americans appeared destined to lose again, the team, which had put its mind and feet to work, displayed that much-needed heart. With thirteen minutes left in the game, Espeseth was charged with a major blunder after she handled the ball in her own penalty box. The Americans had caught a break. Denoncourt whistled a penalty kick, and Akers nailed the shot, energizing the crowd and her teammates. The game appeared destined for overtime.

But the United States came close to winning the game in regulation when Hamm took the ball on a breakaway, using all her speed to charge toward the Norwegian goal before Agnete Carlsen chopped her down from behind. Hamm lay on the ground as Denoncourt pulled out her red card and ejected the Norwegian midfielder.

In overtime, as DiCicco tried to keep his nerves in check, the Americans continued to dominate possession thanks to the player advantage. A win seemed possible. DiCicco made a tactical move and subbed MacMillan into the game in the ninety-sixth minute, replacing a tired Milbrett. The move proved a piece of coaching genius. Less than four minutes after entering the game, MacMillan fielded a pass from Foudy, then kicked the ball from twelve yards out. The shot beat Nordby, setting off a rapturous celebration on the field and in the stands. The United States had exacted its revenge, dethroning the world champions and preventing them from adding a gold medal to their trophy case back in Oslo.

"Never in my wildest dreams," a near-speechless MacMillan exclaimed after the game.[19] As the U.S. players piled on top of Mac-Millan, Akers ran up and down the sidelines waving an oversized American flag as Hamm hugged everyone around her. "I just went crazy. I wanted to hug everyone at once. I was running around in circles," said Hamm.[20]

Norwegian players openly wept as Nordby appeared flummoxed by the goal and ensuing celebrations that took place before her incredulous eyes. "June 17, 1995. It's something we've had in the back of our minds for a year. This team trained on beating [Norway's] defense for more than a year," said DiCicco.[21]

Had it not been for the contract dispute that had plagued the team nine months earlier, MacMillan would have never been on the team. Used by DiCicco as a scab when he was short nine players, MacMillan shined during her brief time in camp. He eventually invited her back and put her on the Olympic roster in time for the Games.

The United States was now in the gold-medal game, but it had to face one more hurdle: China, which recorded a 3–2 win over Brazil in the other semifinal. Whereas Norway settled for the bronze after defeating Brazil 2–0 on August 1 at Sanford Stadium, the United States and China waged their own battle at the same venue some thirty minutes later. A crowd of seventy-six thousand—the largest to ever watch a women's sporting event on American soil—filled the stands. The game had unexpectedly become one of the hottest tickets at the Atlanta Games. It was a watershed moment for women's team sports. The United States' yearlong quest to get back to the top of the soccer world was just ninety minutes away.

DiCicco moved MacMillan into the starting lineup. It paid off once again when she scored after just nineteen minutes. The striker put the ball into the goal after a Hamm shot glanced off Gao's hands and off the left post. China canceled the U.S. lead in the thirty-second minute when Sun Wen chipped the ball over Scurry's head. The ball slowly bounced toward the empty goal, and Chastain streaked across the grass in an attempt to cut off the play but slid into the twine along with the ball.

The game was deadlocked until Milbrett tallied off a pass from Fawcett in the sixty-eighth minute. Hamm, double-teamed all evening, attracted a scrum of defenders each time she touched the ball. As she drew a gaggle of players, Hamm played a perfect through-ball to Fawcett, who centered it to Milbrett, who buried the ball into the back of the net. "Like always, Mia affects a game whether she scores or not. She tears defenses apart. She's the reason we were able to get behind China's defense," said DiCicco.[22]

The U.S. lead held up for twenty-two extremely tense minutes as the Chinese scrambled to tie the score. At the final whistle, DiCicco's players rejoiced. The Americans were Olympic champions after coming up short at the World Cup a year earlier. Scurry made good on her promise later that night by streaking down the streets of Athens—albeit briefly—to the amusement of her teammates.

Aside from winning the gold, the players had become full-fledged trailblazers. Despite the hoopla, NBC, which had aired the Olympics, never showed the game, reducing it to a highlights package. At the Olympics, individuals such as gymnasts, runners, and swimmers had traditionally been celebrated more than teams—and women's soccer became a victim of that narrow broadcast mentality. "NBC still doesn't get it," said Steinbrecher when talking about the television coverage.[23] The team did not appreciate the snub. "The World Cup is great, but the Olympics is what the Americans look at. This is the place for soccer to get the exposure it deserves. This is the stage that people rally around," said Akers.[24]

Not even NBC's refusal to air the game could dampen the players' moods. As the national anthem blared over the loudspeakers, Hamm and her teammates stood proudly atop the podium before a thankful public. With gold medals around their necks, the players stood knowing that they had reached the pinnacle of women's soccer.

NOTES

1. Bill Ward, "U.S. Women's Players Take Stand," *Tampa Tribune*, January 21, 1996, p. 8.
2. Ward, "U.S. Women's Players Take Stand."
3. Ward, "U.S. Women's Players Take Stand."
4. Interview, June 19, 1999.
5. Ward, "U.S. Women's Players Take Stand."
6. Ward, "U.S. Women's Players Take Stand."
7. Interview, June 19, 1999.
8. Interview, June 19, 1999.
9. News conference, July 21, 1996.
10. News conference, July 21, 1996.
11. Jerry Trecker, "There's A Lot Behind U.S. Victory," *Hartford Courant*, July 22, 1996, p. C8.
12. News conference, July 23, 1996.
13. News conference, July 23, 1996.
14. News conference, July 23, 1996.
15. News conference, July 23, 1996.
16. Jere Longman, *The Girls of Summer: The U.S. Women's Soccer Team and How It Changed the World* (New York: HarperCollins, 2001), 176.
17. Longman, *The Girls of Summer*, 177.
18. Longman, *The Girls of Summer*, 178.
19. Ben Smith, "U.S. Women Top Norway, Will Play China for Gold," *Atlanta Journal-Constitution*, July 29, 1996.
20. Don Skwar, "A Goal Is Achieved in Overtime," *Boston Globe*, July 29, 1996.
21. Skwar, "A Goal Is Achieved."
22. News conference, August 1, 1996.
23. Laura Vescey, "Not-Ready-for-TV Women Win Soccer Title," *Seattle Post-Intelligencer*, August 2, 1996.
24. Vescey, "Not-Ready-for-TV."

4

Party Like It's 1999

Hamm had emerged as the world's greatest player and to most American girls—and boys—the model of what a great athlete and soccer player should be. Hamm brought a gift to the game that was a confluence of drama and prodigious talent. From almost the moment she first kicked a ball, something made people want to watch her play.

A mainstay of the national team since the United States won the World Cup in 1991, Hamm became like Michael Jordan. She transcended sport and was discovered by Madison Avenue, who turned her into a pitchwoman for almost every product imaginable, from sports drinks to shampoo.

Hamm made people, even those who never watched soccer, want to flock to stadiums—so much so that attendance records at the United States' games across the country were shattered because of Mia. Dads took their teenage daughters to games to see her, and mothers packed their SUVs with kids. "Hamm-mania" had reached its climax.

Not since the days of Pelé and the North American Soccer League in the mid-1970s had soccer experienced such a surge in popularity in this country. And as trophies and medals piled up, Hamm increasingly became a household name. Hamm was no longer just a soccer player. She was a phenomenon—the start of a new era in women's team sports that put them on par with men.

Hamm's inspiration since childhood was her adopted brother, Garrett, who was in the stands the night she and the United States won the gold medal at the Atlanta Games. "When I was six, my big brother, Garrett, ran circles around me," recalled Hamm.[1] When Hamm was five, her parents adopted Garrett, who was three years older than Mia. "After he joined our family, I followed him wherever he went," recalled Hamm.[2]

Although he was Hamm's biggest supporter, Garrett died in 1997 from complications connected to a bone marrow transplant he underwent to combat a rare blood disease. "It was an extremely difficult time for my family and me, but I was able to persevere through the pain and sorrow with the support of my teammates and the very lessons in courage and fortitude he helped me learn. Garrett was, and will always be, my inspiration," she said (see p. 54).[3]

In 1997, following the Olympics, the team prepared for the 1999 Women's World Cup (to be held in the United States) and went 16–2–0, losing only to Germany and Brazil in exhibition games. In 1998, the team participated in the Goodwill Games in New York City. Once again, the Americans dominated the four-team competition, defeating Denmark 5–0, before winning the competition with a 2–0 victory over China. Against Denmark, Akers scored a spectacular goal, ripping off a thirty-five-yard shot that found its way into the net. During the postgame news conference, a reporter asked if she was surprised that the ball went into the net. Akers leaned forward into the microphone and unabashedly said, "Not very."[4]

In the final against China, both sides were deadlocked 0–0 until the sixty-sixth minute when Lilly placed a perfect pass in Hamm's direction. Hamm did not disappoint, drilling the ball into the left corner for the goal. "I savor that goal because I got one chance near the end of the game and nailed it," said Hamm.[5] Three minutes from the end, with China in desperate need of tying the score, Hamm tallied again, this time from forty yards away following a poor clearance by the Chinese defense. "Those goals were both examples of making the best of what you're offered and using the correct shot to score in each situation," Hamm recalled.[6]

The team's preparation for the 1999 Women's World Cup was on track. The team's success at the Olympics boosted their morale

MIA HAMM

Mia Hamm, whose full name is Mariel Margaret, is to women's soccer what Pelé is to the men's game. A brilliant player and an inspiration to a generation of girls around the country, Hamm scored more goals for the U.S. national team—158—than any other player, male or female, in the history of the sport.

Ironically, Hamm was born with a clubfoot and had to wear corrective shoes as a toddler to help fix the problem. She spent much of her childhood on air force bases, living in Italy for a short time, before moving to Texas. At age fifteen, Hamm became one of the

Photo 4.1. Mia Hamm remains the most famous American soccer player of all time. (Credit: ISI Photos)

youngest players to play for the United States, before going on to attend the University of North Carolina. She helped the Tar Heels win four National Collegiate Athletic Association titles in five years (she sat out the 1991 season to train for the World Cup).

Just nineteen, Hamm was on the team that won the World Cup in 1991. Eight years later, she broke the all-time international goal record, tallying her 158th goal in a game against Brazil. That same year, she lifted the United States to its second World Cup title, adding to the 1996 gold medal she won in Atlanta.

Hamm announced in 2004 that she was retiring at the end of the year, which she capped off by leading the United States to the gold medal at the Olympics in Athens. To honor the feat, the other athletes chose her to be the U.S. delegation's flag bearer during the closing ceremony.

Hamm is widely recognized as one of the best to ever play the sport. She was named one of FIFA's 125 best living players (as chosen by Pelé), and she won the world governing body's World Player of the Year award in 2001 and 2002. In 2007, Hamm was inducted into the National Soccer Hall of Fame. Launched in 2009, the logo for Women's Professional Soccer features Hamm's silhouette.

Hamm was married in 1994 to her college sweetheart Christian Corry, a U.S. Marine Corps pilot, but the couple divorced in 2001. In 2003, Hamm married Boston Red Sox player Nomar Garciaparra. The couple had twin girls, Grace Isabella and Ava Caroline, in 2007.

Appearances: 275
Goals: 158

and that of organizers. FIFA awarded the tournament to the United States, and the organizing committee hoped to capitalize on the team's recent success and Hamm's popularity. The boom also meant that the tournament would be a success, at least when it came to ticket sales.

The goal, of course, was to sell plenty of tickets for the sixteen-team event. The World Cup in Sweden, four years earlier, had been played in small stadiums to modest crowds. The 1999 Women's World Cup organizers had planned to do the same, but the large crowds at the Atlanta Olympics changed everything. Three years later, organizers gambled in hopes that the momentum and buzz created by the U.S. victory would translate into large crowds at cavernous National Football League stadiums across the country. "The ultimate challenge is to go out and get lots of people in the stands. We want players to play before huge crowds and that is something we can never lose focus of," said Steinbrecher.[7]

Marla Messing, president of the 1999 Women's World Cup organizing committee, agreed that attracting fans was its first priority: "While we don't have the Olympic name attached to us, we will have the World Cup name attached to us and we think that's just as important and meaningful to the American public."[8]

The original plan was to stage the tournament along the East Coast at a few small venues holding no more than fifteen thousand spectators. Only the final would be held at the fifty-six-thousand-seat RFK Stadium in Washington, D.C. Organizers scrapped that plan and opted to play the tournament opener at Giants Stadium, just outside New York. A gamble? Maybe. The organizers, however, believed that it was one worth the risk. The large venue, once the home of the legendary New York Cosmos and used at the 1994 World Cup, was about to make history again. The final would be played at another large and famous venue: the Rose Bowl in Pasadena, California. "We decided this would be a great place to begin," Steinbrecher said of Giants Stadium.[9]

Critics argued that the crowds the U.S. team got at the Olympics were due to the desire of fans to attend the Olympics and, in this case, settling for a ticket to just about any event. Trying to stage soccer games at large venues, the critics added, would result in the nearly impossible task of having to fill seats and a potential embarrassment in the end.

Organizers proved the soccer haters wrong. The June 19 opener at Giants Stadium sold out within weeks. For the Americans' debut against Denmark, all seventy-seven thousand seats were taken—setting a new record for a U.S. women's game. At the start of the tournament, organizers had sold more than 460,000 tickets, eclipsing the 300,000 tickets sold just a few months earlier for the women's NCAA basketball tournament, traditionally considered the marquee event for women's sports in this country.

Getting the word out that the United States was even hosting the World Cup began in 1997 when organizers set up tents across the country over a quiet Columbus Day weekend. Passersby in several cities, such as New York and Los Angeles, were handed bumper stickers with the tournament's official logo, featuring a running woman with a ponytail bouncing in the wind, in the hopes that word of mouth would be the engine that would create interest.

Six months later, the committee mailed out nearly one million brochures to fans and coaches hoping to get the word out. By the end of 1998, organizers had sold two hundred thousand tickets without spending any money on a television- or billboard-based advertising. Soccer moms and their daughters were not the only target, said Messing, but men as well. As shown by the 1994 World Cup and the launch of Major League Soccer two years later (the first U.S. men's pro league since the demise of the NASL in 1985), there was a real thirst for soccer by American sports fans and the many ethnic groups who immigrated to the United States. Organizers were hopeful that if the United States reached the July 10 final, they could sell out the 92,542 seats that were available for the match. By comparison, 113,000 tickets were sold for the entire 1995 Women's World Cup in Sweden. The 1999 Women's World Cup would also be played at Soldier Field, Chicago; Foxboro Stadium, outside Boston; Stanford Stadium in Palo Alto, California; Civic Stadium, in Portland, Oregon; Spartan Stadium, in San Jose, California; and Jack Kent Cooke Stadium, in Landover, Maryland.

Those who feared that the women's soccer revolution would not be televised need not have worried. Whereas NBC showed only highlights of the U.S. gold-medal victory, ABC/ESPN would telecast all thirty-two games at the World Cup, with FIFA estimating a world-wide international audience of one billion. This would truly be the biggest stage ever for women's soccer. It would be bigger than any previous World Cup and larger than the Olympic soccer tournament.

With an overall budget of just $30 million—about one-tenth that for the male version of the World Cup—the 1999 Women's World Cup organizers had limited funds at their disposal. Getting the message out would not be easy. Corporate sponsors pitched in only $6 million, a paltry amount compared to the estimated $50 million typically amassed by the men's quadrennial tournament. Nevertheless, in a bid to grow interest, Messing put together a viable business plan that limited ad spending and capitalized on America's hunger for top-notch soccer, regardless of gender.

The organizing committee knew that the tournament's success hinged on a U.S. success. Should the Americans not reach the final, interest in the tournament would wane and thus turn into a both a public relations failure and a financial disaster for organizers. Interest would then be relegated to moms and dads and their suburban teenage girls, a group that formed the core grassroots support of the U.S. team. It was teenage girls who mobbed U.S. players after games, turning postgame autograph sessions into a shrieking frenzy reminiscent of a boy-band concert.

The U.S. players—knowing that the pressure was on them—were nonetheless excited about playing at home. "This is the biggest women's soccer event ever in this country. We couldn't be happier. We'll never forget the Olympics, but we hope to put on a great show once again," said Lilly.[10]

Headaches faced by organizers were not limited to whether the United States would advance to the tournament's latter stages. They also feared that China would threaten to withdraw in the wake of the inadvertent U.S. bombing of the Chinese embassy in Belgrade, in May 1999, during air raids over Yugoslavia. However, the Chinese, relishing the opportunity to defeat the Americans on their home turf, decided not to pull out. The Chinese players arrived in the United States as scheduled, before the start of the tournament to adapt to the climate and conditions. Some thirty Chinese journalists followed their every move. Another two hundred million viewers in China watched their team's games.

Another fear involved the totalitarian nation North Korea, another qualifier out of the Asian group and, in general, a mystery to many because of its international isolation. Organizers feared that the North Korean players would be denied visas by the State Department, but that never materialized. If anything, North Korea was eager to come to America's shores. Not known for its soccer, the women's team traveled to the United States as an underdog. Once here, several players complained of toothaches, and FIFA ensured that the players received free dental treatment at the hands of American dentists.

DiCicco also had his worries. In July 1998, with the World Cup a year away, the team was divided on an issue that had reverberations across women's sports. Debbie Keller, a member of the national team, filed a sexual-harassment lawsuit against Dorrance, her coach at the University of North Carolina from 1993 to 1996. Dorrance was one of the most respected women's soccer coaches in the country. He was now being accused by Keller of making unwanted romantic advances. Keller alleged that Dorrance regularly engaged in inappropriate physical contact with the players by touching their bodies and would "constantly interrogate" players about their personal lives.[11] Keller's lawsuit said that the school was "aware that it was rumored that Dorrance had resigned from his position as [U.S. coach] because he had engaged in a sexual relationship with a player on the women's national team"—a player who was never publicly identified.[12] Steinbrecher, the federation's executive director, said that there was "no truth whatsoever" to those rumors.[13]

Dorrance denied both the rumors and that he had engaged in any inappropriate behavior with his players. To make matters worse, another former Tar Heels player, Melissa Jennings, joined in on the lawsuit. She alleged that Dorrance encouraged underage drinking and that he once pressured her to withdraw $400 from the bank to help pay for team supplies.[14]

The school stood by Dorrance, as did Hamm and other former players, who signed a letter saying that he and his coaching staff behaved "appropriately and with absolute professionalism and integrity" and that they had "no reservations about our own daughters someday playing soccer" at North Carolina.[15]

Other than Dorrance, the U.S. team had the most to lose as the lawsuit unfolded. Of the eventual twenty players who made DiCicco's final roster, eight had been coached by Dorrance at North Carolina. Some players were sympathetic with Keller. Others upset at her. Either way, the tension was omnipresent. Nerves were frayed as the team prepared for the World Cup—a distraction that DiCicco did not need. "You're going to have personal feelings, and they're going to be real. The legal entity is going to take its course," DiCicco assured the players during a team meeting.[16] DiCicco told Overbeck, who had also played for Dorrance, that she had to put her personal feelings aside and "hold the team together."[17]

In October 1998, DiCicco cut Keller from the team, citing "chemistry issues" with her teammates.[18] Used mostly as a sub, Keller had been the second-leading scorer for the United States that year with fourteen goals. By the time the invitations to join training camp in January 1999 were sent out, Keller was not one of the players to get one. She was livid. She alleged that she had been punished for suing Dorrance, and she filed a lawsuit seeking to be reinstated. She also alleged in her suit that Dorrance still had enough influence over DiCicco and the federation that they had been persuaded to drop her from the team.[19]

The team eventually released a statement saying that it would not speak publicly about the Keller lawsuit. The players, however, continued to talk privately about it. The lawsuit split the team. Some believed Keller. Others sided with Dorrance. Then there were others who believed that Keller should have remained on the team. "I think anyone with that much productivity, hands down, should have been there in camp," said Milbrett.[20]

Akers, who had played for Dorrance at the 1991 World Cup, wrote letters of support to both her former coach and Keller. "I can see both sides. Keller is a good player, she scores goals. However, the situation she put herself in was a potential distraction and divider among the team," said Akers.[21]

The issue also divided two team veterans. Hamm and Chastain, who were roommates, had it out in January 1999 during the start of training camp. Hamm had been a staunch Dorrance supporter, whereas Chastain had her own history with him. Chastain feuded with Dorrance when she was not invited to training camp and eventually left off the World Cup team by DiCicco in 1995. "In the end, everyone had their own opinion. We all had different relationships with those involved. That's not a bad thing," said Hamm.[22]

On May 10, 1999, the American Arbitration Association rejected Keller's complaint, siding with DiCicco. Keller, who led Fortuna Hjorring to the Danish league title, was left on the outside looking in. Dorrance was also eventually cleared of any wrongdoing when a judge threw out the lawsuit in 2004. A year later, Dorrance was elected to the North Carolina Sports Hall of Fame.

With the scandal seemingly behind them, the team could not wait to sink its teeth into its opponents, starting with Denmark before a packed house at Giants Stadium. At the hotel before the opening game against the Danes, the players performed an impromptu dance party in the hallway. "We were just a bunch of girls acting wacky, singing and trying to work off some nervous energy," said Hamm.[23]

As the team bus made its twenty-five-minute trip from Manhattan to East Rutherford, New Jersey, the car traffic stretching from the Lincoln Tunnel to Giants Stadium was more reminiscent of a football game than a soccer match. The jitters that the players had tried to dance off suddenly came back. They pressed their faces against the bus windows, gazing in amazement as they slowly navigated through bumper-to-bumper traffic. The sellout they had only heard about materialized in front of their eyes. Families set up tailgate parties in the sprawling parking lot, and girls and boys kicked around soccer balls. "This is the place where some of the world's biggest events have taken place. Everyone has heard of Giants Stadium. Now women's soccer can also claim a special place here," said Chastain.[24]

Once inside the packed stadium, the crowd—the largest to ever watch a women's sporting event in this country—chanted "USA! USA!" for the duration of the game. "I know it gave me goose bumps. How could you not," Hamm said of the reception she and her teammates received that afternoon.[25]

The players knew that when they stepped onto the grass field at Giants Stadium for this World Cup, things would be drastically different from the way they were at the 1991 tournament, when the team won it all in China and returned home to a largely disinterested public, and in 1995, when it was eliminated before a small crowd in Sweden with few people back home caring.

The game itself was an afterthought as the Americans downed Denmark, 3–0, with goals from Hamm, Foudy, and Lilly, before a pro-U.S. crowd. "We're all going to remember this day for the rest of our lives. It's wonderful to play before such great support," said Hamm.[26] Chastain said the crowd reaction that day will forever be etched in her mind. "We walked through the shadowy tunnel . . . and stepped out into the bright sunlight. A huge roar burst from the capacity crowd. The flashing of thousands of cameras exploded before our eyes, and the smell of the fresh-cut grass was heavy in the air. [The World Cup] was all finally happening," she recalled.[27]

Hamm's goal, the 110th of her career, before a sea of American flags came after seventeen minutes when she put away a powerful volley past Danish goalkeeper Dorthe Larsen. "Mia was truly awesome. Truly awesome," said DiCicco.[28]

Denmark tried to surprise the U.S. defense with several counterattacks, but Scurry was able to shut them down. The game's outcome was still in doubt until Foudy scored off a long cross from Hamm with seventeen minutes left to play. Lilly put the game away with a shot from twenty yards out with a minute left to cap off the win. "Opponents can try to stop us for a half, but they can't keep us off the scoreboard for the whole game," said Scurry.[29]

The Americans, now atop group A with three points, had to prepare to play Nigeria five days later in Chicago. DiCicco, privately hoping that Hamm could again spearhead the attack with a goal or two, publicly said that expecting a striker to score in every game is a tall order. Although Hamm was in the midst of a seven-game scoring streak entering the Nigeria game, DiCicco was focused on assembling a strong defense. "No player can score a goal a game for long stretches, not if you're playing at a high level. I'd love for Mia to [score goals], but we can't expect that in this World Cup," said DiCicco.[30]

The game against Nigeria would not only decide who took first place (following Nigeria's 2–1 win over North Korea on June 23) but also determine who would earn a berth to the quarterfinals. The Americans knew that a pro-U.S. crowd would show up at Solider Field to back them.

On June 24, the United States took on Nigeria before an enthusiastic crowd of more than sixty-five thousand, many decked out in red, white, and blue. The African champions wasted no time getting on the board, putting the Americans in a 1–0 hole with a goal from Nkiru Okosieme after just two minutes. Foudy's poor clearance had allowed striker Mercy Akide to scoop up the ball and dish off a pass to Okosieme, who drilled a low shot into the corner past Scurry.

Two minutes later, Chastain and Overbeck collided in the box, allowing Okosieme another close-in shot that went wide. "Giving up a goal in the second minute was not a good start for us, but then things started picking up for us," said Lilly.[31]

Nigeria proved totally unable to contain the American offense. Forward Cindy Parlow had her attempt for the top left corner stopped following an acrobatic save by goalkeeper Ann Chiejine in the eleventh minute. Two minutes later Chastain sent a twelve-yard flying header off the crossbar. Then the Nigerians' luck ran out with the U.S. recording six unanswered goals within a twenty-three-minute span, including three in a four-minute span to take a 3–1 lead. The tying tally came on an own goal in the nineteenth minute after Hamm slid a pass in front of the goal and defender Ifeanyichukwu Chiejene, in a bid to stop Akers, had the ball come off her foot and into the net. A minute later, it was Hamm who was the recipient of a pass from Lilly. Hamm carried into the top right of the box before sending a fifteen-yard shot into the top near corner to put the United States ahead 2–1. "I just shot hard. That's the kind of shot that if it goes in, you're celebrating. If not, it's a bad decision," said Hamm.[32]

In the twenty-third minute, Parlow fed Milbrett, whose short blast went off Chiejine's right hand and into the right corner to make it 3–1. In the thirty-second minute, Lilly converted a pass from Hamm, and seven minutes later Foudy found Akers, who headed the ball from five yards out to make it 5–1.

In the forty-second minute, Milbrett sent a pass across field to the left side of the penalty box where Chastain nodded it back to Parlow, who roofed a header from six yards out. Milbrett finished the scoring in the eighty-third minute, taking a pass from Parlow, to end the 7-1 rout.

The players greeted each other with high fives as they walked off the field. DiCicco had a look of relief on his face. His team had not only won but won big after falling behind early. The World Cup darlings had demonstrated a lot of character in their biggest tournament victory since downing Taiwan en route to their 1991 World Cup run. "Everyone just refocused. Six goals later, it was a different story," said Hamm.[33]

The physical game against Nigeria left the players nursing an array of injuries. "After getting beat up by the Nigerians, we needed every minute [of rest]. Some of the starters didn't even practice the next day when we got to Boston," said Hamm.[34]

With a berth to the quarterfinals wrapped up, the final group game, against North Korea on June 27 at Foxboro Stadium, was a formality. DiCicco used the game to rest some of his players. Although the game was not a sellout, the first featuring the United States at this competition, organizers did take time out to announce that a whopping 560,000 tickets had been sold.

With the game scoreless at halftime, DiCicco changed course and threw some stars at the North Korean defense. With Milbrett coming in for Hamm and Foudy for Parlow, the subs entered the game in the second half, sparking the United States to a 3–0 victory to finish first in the group, with nine points.

In the fifty-sixth minute, MacMillan's dipping shot from just outside the box, off a well-placed Foudy pass, got past goalkeeper Kye Yonh Sun at the near post. The goal put the Americans ahead and the fifty-thousand fans into a tizzy. Until that point, the North

Korean defense had stymied the American offense and thwarted every offensive effort as a worried DiCicco looked on from the sidelines.

The teams traded shots—both of which hit the woodwork—as the game grew in intensity. Lilly's powerful left-footed shot slammed against the post. The North Koreans returned the favor when Jin Pyol Hui's shot from fifteen yards out thumped the crossbar.

The Americans put the game away in the sixty-eighth minute after a long run from Milbrett, who passed the ball off to MacMillan in the box. That is when MacMillan provided a soft pass in the air for Venturini, who headed the ball into the goal. Venturini scored again eight minutes later with another header off a MacMillan pass for the 3–0 win. The United States had landed in the quarterfinals with a perfect record. Up next for DiCicco's team was Germany, which finished second in Group B with a win and two ties.

The quarterfinal clash took place on July 1 at Jack Kent Cooke Stadium in Landover, Maryland, before a crowd of fifty thousand, which included President Bill Clinton and his wife, Hillary. The Germans proved to be the United States' toughest opponent at this tournament. The team started off slow, and the Germans made them pay. Down 2–1 at halftime, the United States came out roaring in the second period. Once the players put the squandered chances of the first half behind them, the United States tied the score with Chastain in the forty-ninth minute off a Hamm corner kick.

In the sixty-sixth minute, Fawcett, who hung back for most of the game, was well positioned on another U.S. corner, and assisted MacMillan, who headed the ball past goalkeeper Silke Rottenberg. "I knew [MacMillan] was going to the near post because that's where she likes to put the ball," Fawcett said.[35]

DiCicco's emphasis on set pieces in practice had paid off. His move to put in MacMillan just moments before the United States won the corner kick proved a stroke of coaching genius. Fawcett said that after she struck the ball, she "knew it was going in. I just knew it." The United States was ahead 3–2, but it did not stop there.[36]

The team locked down its defense and thwarted Germany's feeble attempts to tie the score and push the game into overtime. The final whistle brought with it the customary victory lap and a look of relief on the players' faces. "They had great timing and position on set pieces. We just needed to wake up," said Germany coach Tina Theune-Mayer.[37]

Hamm, who suffered a hip injury in practice two days before the Germany game, chalked up the win to heart. "We've found a different way to win each game. Against Germany, it was all heart."[38]

The victory gave the United States an automatic berth to the 2000 Sydney Olympics and set up a Fourth of July clash in Palo Alto, California, against Brazil, who had defeated Nigeria 4–3 in overtime. In the other semifinal, China was pitted against Norway.

The Brazil game was a rematch of sorts for the United States. In 1994, the U.S. men's team played Brazil at the World Cup, on the same day and in the same stadium. The Americans lost a tight match 1–0. The Brazilians went on to win the World Cup.

DiCicco's team did not want a repeat of history. This time, the Americans were favored. They were the ones expected to play for the title at the Rose Bowl, not Brazil. With a strong sun beating down on the Stanford Stadium field, the United States and Brazil squared off.

The United States got on the board after just five minutes, with the complicity of Brazilian goalie Maravilha. A Foudy cross from deep on the right flank went straight toward Maravilha, who watched as the ball deflected off her fingers and in Parlow's direction. She wasted no time heading the ball into the net for the goal. "It definitely took the pressure off. We were able to sit back a little after the goal instead of having to worry that Brazil could score first and we'd have to play catch-up," said Parlow.[39]

Brazil, however, came back with a vengeance, peppering Scurry with shot after shot as the U.S. defense tried frantically to clear balls and keep possession away from its opponents. The Brazilians almost tied the match in the thirtieth minute, but Scurry made a diving save to stop Pretinha's shot. A few minutes later, a Pretinha cross almost made its way into the net, but on that occasion it was Akers who cleared the ball off the line.

It was a controversial foul on Hamm late in the game that sealed Brazil's fate. A goal kick taken by Overbeck was headed downfield by Akers. Hamm latched on to the ball and ran it into the box in an attempt to score. That is when Hamm was nudged by Brazilian captain Elaine and went down. Without hesitation, the referee awarded the United States a penalty kick. Akers scored on the ensuing kick in the eightieth minute for the 2–0 win.

In the other semifinal, played the same day in Boston, China defeated Norway 5–0, setting up a final against the United States in a rematch of the 1996 gold-medal game. The final was played on July 10 at a Rose Bowl filled with a little more than ninety-thousand fans turning up to watch this scintillating rivalry, with another forty million viewers watching on television sets across the country. The fans in attendance surpassed the record for a women's soccer game, set just three weeks earlier in the World Cup opener at Giants Stadium. The enthusiasm in the stands topped that of the 1996 Olympic gold-medal match with fans arriving early, decked out in face paint and chanting "USA! USA!"

The United States and China were clearly the best two teams at the tournament. China outscored opponents 19–2, whereas the United States did so by an 18–3 margin. The American fans were revved up following the national anthem, which was punctuated by a U.S. Navy F-18 flyover.

There was not much to cheer about after that. The game was a sloppy, drawn-out affair with neither defense tested much. The biggest reaction from the crowd was when President Clinton was shown on the scoreboard. The game ended scoreless following ninety minutes of regulation and thirty minutes of sudden-death overtime. The game was headed to penalty kicks (photo 4.2).

The United States would have never forced penalties without the clutch performance from Lilly. With the ninety-degree heat beating down on the field, Lilly was able to head the ball off the line in overtime after Fan Yunjie's header beat Scurry and appeared headed for the back of the net. The play drew a loud gasp, followed by loud cheers. The goal would have won the game for China.

Turning in an equally brilliant performance was Akers. At thirty-three, she was the oldest player on DiCicco's team. She was forced to leave the game in the final minutes of regulation after smacking into Scurry on a Chinese corner kick. Akers was replaced by Sara Whalen. Akers, plagued by chronic fatigue, had fallen to the turf, feeling woozy and struggling to get up. She was taken to the locker room and fed fluids intravenously. She struggled to follow the game on a small television and pulled herself up to watch only during the shootout.

Photo 4.2. Michelle Akers (no. 10) and her teammates do their best to defend against a Chinese free kick. (Credit: ISI Photos)

Every great athlete has a defining moment in his or her career—a game, a play, a shot—that will be forever immortalized as the defining moment in that player's life. Sometimes, it takes years to pinpoint that moment. Other times, you recognize it the instant it happens. Chastain was to become that player. She had always worked hard and sacrificed herself for the sake of the team. Unselfish and relentless with the ball for much of the tournament, Chastain was a locker-room favorite and had emerged as one of the team's leaders.

Chastain was not even supposed to line up for one of the penalty kicks. Not originally. In the dying minutes of overtime, DiCicco glanced over at assistant coach Lauren Gregg and asked her to jot down the names of the players who looked best suited to convert during the much-dreaded shootout. Gregg wrote down five names. Chastain wasn't one of them. She was listed sixth and would only be used should the shootout reach sudden death. She had injured her right foot and Gregg did not want to chance it.

Days earlier, DiCicco watched as Chastain banged kick after kick into the goal during practice. If she were to kick fifth—the decisive kick—she would have to use her much weaker, left foot. DiCicco amended Gregg's list, moving Chastain up a spot. DiCicco knew that Chastain would be up to the task. Hamm, who was fourth to kick, tried to get DiCicco to scratch her name off the list altogether, imploring him to use MacMillan. DiCicco refused. He had no choice given that he had already handed the list to the referee.

Tied 2–2 in the shootout, Scurry saved Liu Ying's shot, diving with her outstretched arms to make the stop. "I read the kick pretty well. She hit it hard, but I don't think she placed it that well," said Scurry.[40] Lilly scored to put the United States ahead, and Zhang Ouying and Hamm traded goals.

Tied 4–4 with one kick left, Chastain placed the ball on the spot. She slowly walked away from the ball, keeping her eyes fixed on the ball and avoiding staring at the crowd behind the goal or Gao.

Chastain blasted the ball past Gao, and the fans jumped to their feet in unison. Her teammates, standing in the midfield circle, exulted. They sprinted toward Chastain to embrace her. In one of the greatest spontaneous celebrations in sports history, Chastain peeled off her sweat-soaked jersey to reveal a black sports bra (photo 4.3).

Photo 4.3. **Brandi Chastain and her shirtless celebration made the cover of *Sports Illustrated, Time,* and *Newsweek* all in the same week. (Credit: ISI Photos)**

As the crowd cheered, the players hugged Chastain, piling on top of her in unabashed joy. Chastain's celebration became the symbol of the team's triumph, splashed on the cover of newspapers and magazines across the country. "It was obviously a wonderful moment, but I do wish more attention could be paid to the many other things my team and I have done. They add up to a lot more than a penalty kick celebration," said Chastain, who grew up admiring English soccer superstar George Best.[41]

The Chinese players hung their heads in disbelief. The Americans were once again world champions (photo 4.4).

"I'm delighted we won this tournament. It came down to them not allowing themselves to lose. It's a storybook ending to a team that has a place in history," said DiCicco.[42]

Photo 4.4. U.S. captain Carla Overbeck lifts the 1999 Women's World Cup at the Rose Bowl, surrounded by her teammates as FIFA president Sepp Blatter (left) looks on in delight. (Credit: ISI Photos)

NOTES

1. Mia Hamm, *Go for the Goal: A Champion's Guide to Winning in Soccer and Life* (New York: HarperCollins, 1999), 3.

2. Hamm, *Go for the Goal*, 11.

3. Hamm, *Go for the Goal*, 12.

4. News conference, July 25, 1998.

5. Hamm, *Go for the Goal*, 145.

6. Hamm, *Go for the Goal*, 145–146.

7. News conference, March 19, 1997.

8. News conference, March 19, 1997.

9. News conference, November 19, 1997.

10. Interview, November 19, 1997.

11. Jere Longman, *The Girls of Summer: The U.S. Women's Soccer Team and How It Changed the World* (New York: HarperCollins, 2001), 180–181.

12. Longman, *The Girls of Summer*, 181.

13. Longman, *The Girls of Summer*, 181.

14. Longman, *The Girls of Summer*, 181.

15. Longman, *The Girls of Summer*, 181.

16. Longman, *The Girls of Summer*, 182.

17. Longman, *The Girls of Summer*, 183.

18. Longman, *The Girls of Summer*, 183.

19. Longman, *The Girls of Summer*, 183.

20. Longman, *The Girls of Summer*, 184.

21. Longman, *The Girls of Summer*, 185.

22. Interview, June 19, 1999.

23. Hamm, *Go for the Goal*, 215.

24. Interview, June 19, 1999.

25. Interview, June 19, 1999.

26. Interview, June 19, 1999.

27. Brandi Chastain, *It's Not about the Bra* (New York: HarperCollins, 2004), 175.

28. Interview, June 19, 1999.

29. Interview, June 19, 1999.

30. Grant Wahl, "High Hopes: As Mia Hamm Got the U.S. in the World Cup, Was Too Much Expected of Her," *CNNSI.com*, June 22, 1999 (accessed September 13, 2007).

31. News conference, June 24, 1999.

32. News conference, June 24, 1999.

33. News conference, June 24, 1999.

34. Hamm, *Go for the Goal*, 221.

35. News conference, July 1, 1999.

36. News conference, July 1, 1999.

37. News conference, July 1, 1999.
38. Interview, July 1, 1999.
39. News conference, July 4, 1999.
40. News conference, July 10, 1999.
41. Chastain, *It's Not about the Bra*, xvii.
42. News conference, July 10, 1999

5

Feeling Down Under

Following the magnificent triumph at the World Cup, many questions swirled around the team as they prepared for the 2000 Sydney Olympics. Would DiCicco return? Would Akers be back?

DiCicco deserved a lot of credit for rebuilding the team from its third-place World Cup finish in 1995 and developing a more diversified attack—and the federation knew it. He realized that the Americans could not just depend on physical abilities, as they had before, to overcome such technically gifted opponents as China, Norway, and Brazil. Akers's gutsy attitude and experience, meanwhile, would be hard to replace. She maintained possession in the United States' defensive half like no other player and distributed the ball well offensively, allowing Fawcett and Chastain to move forward.

The answer to both questions was no. DiCicco left. So did Akers. Despite that, the United States entered the Sydney Games the odds-on favorite to win the gold medal. Adding to the crop of veterans that had won the World Cup was a new generation of gifted youngsters, such as forwards Aly Wagner and Danielle Fotopoulos.

Although the college ranks were the place DiCicco could look to for talent, the federation and the players knew that the only way that the national team could remain successful was with the implementation of a pro women's league. Development of a league ultimately rested on whether there were enough sponsorship dollars to develop a viable business plan. The National Soccer Alliance made efforts in 1997, which had the support of the top players. It developed a business plan that was designed to have a league in operation in 1998. Nike and Reebok even expressed interest in becoming sponsors. Despite that, the league was never launched.

U.S. Soccer officials were not enthusiastic, calling the creation of a women's league premature. Others thought that it would hurt the development of Major League Soccer (MLS), a pro men's league launched in 1996. For a time, there was the danger that two women's leagues would be formed—one headed by John Hendricks, CEO of Discovery Corporation, and another by MLS. The men's league already had an operation up and running, but the Hendricks proposal was backed by $40 million from major media companies. Fortunately for the growth of the women's game, MLS backed off, and Hendricks was able to get sanctioning by U.S. Soccer for his Women's United Soccer Association (WUSA) with a partnership agreement between WUSA and MLS, promising to work to the benefit of both parties.

Eight cities were awarded franchises, and when compared to MLS's rocky launch, the WUSA got off the ground smoothly in 2001. The league signed nearly the entire national team roster, and through the draft, many of the world's top stars. When the league finally debuted in the spring of 2001, the final piece of the puzzle was completed for the U.S. women's program.

With a women's league set to commence in a year's time, the U.S. team trained for the 2000 Sydney Olympics. The Americans were the reigning World and Olympic champions, and it was not likely that anyone would knock Hamm and her teammates off that perch. That did not mean that challengers such as Norway and China were not going to try.

U.S. Soccer, meanwhile, signed April Heinrichs, an assistant under DiCicco, to replace him. DiCicco had decided to retire from the national team. Heinrichs, who played on the U.S. team that won the 1991 World Cup, became the first woman to coach the team.

The team entered the Olympics at a disadvantage following a less-than-favorable draw. The United States was in Group F and would open the tournament against Norway on September 14 in

Melbourne, one of several venues outside Sydney used for soccer during the Olympics. The team would then play China three days later and Nigeria on September 20. The draw ensured that at least one of the best teams in the world (the United States, Norway, and China) would not advance to the medal round, given that only two teams from each group would reach the semifinals. Meanwhile, host Australia, whose team was not expected to contend for a medal, was placed in Group E, with Germany, Sweden, and Brazil. "We very much respect Norway, China and Nigeria, and understand that this is a game full of adversity, but I'm confident that we have the team that can handle any challenge to again become the best team in the world," said Heinrichs.[1]

With a month to go before the Olympics, Heinrichs named her eighteen-player roster. There were no surprises. Fifteen members of the 1999 World Cup team were on the roster, with three players making their debut at an international tournament. Heinrichs called up goalkeeper Siri Mullinix, defender Danielle Slaton, and midfielder Nikki Serlenga.

Akers would have made the team at age thirty-four had she not decided to retire. On August 24, 2000, Akers announced that she was calling it quits. A nagging shoulder injury and battle with chronic fatigue syndrome ended Akers's dream of playing in her fifth world competition. "After winning the gold medal in 1996, I promised myself to never again play in the condition I was in during those Olympic Games. . . . This year was no exception, and after the 1999 World Cup, I wrestled for months about whether to play or not, but eventually decided to go for it because I knew unless I was absolutely sure I had spent every possible ounce of myself trying to play, I would beat myself up with second guessing for the rest of my life," said Akers, who retired after tallying 105 goals in 153 international appearances.[2]

The team had to temporarily do without Overbeck, who was slow to recover from a knee injury and the effects of Graves disease, a thyroid disorder that is nonthreatening but causes fatigue and rapid weight loss. She was diagnosed with the disorder earlier in the year and was forced to miss training camp in San Diego.

As much as the team would miss Akers, Heinrichs knew that they had to move forward. The Olympics were just weeks away, and the team was headed down the final stretch in preparation. The United

States entered the Summer Games with a 22–4–7 record—with all four losses coming against Norway. Lorrie Fair, a benchwarmer on the 1999 World Cup team, took Akers's place.

Under Heinrichs, the team underwent a transformation. She changed the U.S. formation from DiCicco's offensive-minded 4–3–3 to a more defensive-oriented 4–4–2. Fawcett moved from right back to the center of defense, where she joined Kate Sobrero. Christie Pearce took the place of Overbeck in Fawcett's previous position on the right. Behind them was Mullinix, who was quicker than Scurry but lacked the big international match experience that every team needs in a goalkeeper at big tournaments. How well she could play under pressure would go a long way in determining how well the United States would do in Australia. The rest of the team consisted of familiar names. Foudy was turned into a holding midfielder under Heinrichs. Lilly, who was stuck in a yearlong scoring drought, continued to hold down her place in the left part of the midfield. MacMillan moved to the right flank. Up front, Hamm continued to weave her magic as the world's best female player. She partnered with Milbrett.

Despite the firepower, Heinrich's formation yielded little in the way of goals. The team's 4–0 win over Brazil on September 1 in the final pre-Olympic tune-up in San Jose was seen as a sign that the United States' scoring ability had returned. In the two games before the Brazil match (against Russia and Canada), the United States scored only two goals. Both those games ended in 1–1 draws against opponents that the United States had regularly routed.

NBC once again held the U.S. broadcasting rights to the Olympics. Unlike the four years earlier, this time the network decided to air all the U.S. team's games on its cable affiliates MSNBC and CNBC.

The U.S. opened the tournament against Norway—never an easy game for the Americans. In it, Heinrichs started Hamm and Milbrett on attack, and the pair eased any fear of not scoring goals. Norway had the first chance to score, two minutes into the game, as Monica Knudsen ran onto a pass from Dagny Mellgren for a strike on goal but poorly played the ball and it rolled wide left. The Americans took over from there, earning three corner kicks in the first three minutes while establishing an attacking rhythm that kept the Norwegians on the defensive the whole game.

Milbrett used her speed to run circles around Norway's defenders. The combination of Milbrett's speed and Mullinix's powerful punting created the first goal in the eighteenth minute. Mullinix came thirty-five yards out of her net to clear a rolling ball, sending a booming kick fifty yards up the field that put Milbrett in a footrace with the Norwegian defense.

Milbrett snagged the ball and pushed her way between defenders Anne Tonnesson and Brit Sandaune as she headed the bouncing ball toward goal. Milbrett's speed separated her from the defenders near the penalty box, but the sliding Bente Nordby got a piece of her first shot from fifteen yards out. The ball slipped under the Norwegian goalkeeper, and Milbrett ran down the deflection to shoot again from seven yards, tucking the ball into the open net for the 1–0 lead.

The United States got a scare in the twenty-third minute when Mullinix missed a save, but Christine Pearce was in good position and cleared the ball away from danger. Despite that, Mullinix played well in her tournament debut.

A minute later, Hamm added a second goal. Lilly (see next page) sent a short pass from the top of the penalty area over the Norwegian defense to Hamm, who perfectly timed her run to avoid the offside trap. Lilly's soft touch put Hamm free on goal along the left side of the box, allowing her to shoot the ball into the net from ten yards out.

The United States got off to a dream start, and Heinrichs could not have been happier. "It was a great way to start a tough tournament like this and really gives us a boost of confidence. We have the ultimate respect for Norway," she said.[3]

On September 17, the United States took on China in Melbourne. A win would put the Americans through to the medal round. China, coming off a victory over Nigeria, was in the same position and in search of a victory. The rematch of the World Cup final had promised to be a riveting affair. Instead, the game turned out to be one of missed opportunities for the United States.

Foudy put the United States ahead in the thirty-eighth minute on a header that beat Gao. Foudy, swarmed by six defenders, jumped higher than the rest and scored from just six yards out. The United States tried to build on its lead before halftime with three good chances. In the fortieth minute, MacMillan chased down a pass along the right side of the box and then slid to send a delicate chip

KRISTINE LILLY

In the history of the U.S. program, Kristine Lilly has played for the team the longest. A national team career that began in 1987, Lilly, nicknamed the "Iron Woman" for her longevity as a player, remains an active member of the squad and the team's all-time appearance leader.

Lilly, who attended Wilton High School in Wilton, Connecticut, played for the University of North Carolina and won the Hermann Trophy in 1991 along with four National Collegiate Athletic Association titles.

Photo 5.1.   Kristine Lilly has played for the United States since 1987 and at age thirty-six played at the 2007 Women's World Cup. (Credit: ISI Photos)

Since 1991, Lilly has played in every major tournament for the United States, with the exception being the 2008 Beijing Olympics, owing to the birth of her daughter. She is a two-time World Cup winner and a two-time Olympic gold medalist. She reached the amazing milestone of two hundred caps in 2000 and three hundred in 2006.

A midfielder who captained the U.S. squad at the 2007 World Cup, Lilly became the first woman to play at five World Cups. At age thirty-six, she became the oldest player to ever score a goal at the World Cup, when she tallied against England on September 22, 2007. After missing the 2008 Olympics, Lilly returned to the team and retired in 2010.

Lilly is married and has a daughter, Sidney Marie Heavey.

Appearances: 352
Goals: 130

to the far post, but Lilly drove her shot straight into the arms of Gao from a sharp angle. A minute later, Lilly weaved her way through two Chinese defenders and struck a low but hard shot from fifteen yards out that Gao saved. In the forty-third minute, MacMillan spun another cross in from the right flank, bending the ball behind the defense as Hamm jumped in the air to attempt a header, but a lunging Chinese defender got a piece of the ball that sailed over the end line.

In the second half, the Chinese buzzed around the U.S. goal in search of an equalizer. Although Fawcett and Chastain did a wonderful job temporarily repelling the Chinese attack, they could do nothing to stop China from tying the score. When China won a free kick from thirty yards out in the sixty-seventh minute, the defense could do nothing to stop Sun from scoring. Mullinix flew to the upper corner and got a palm on the ball but was unable to save it as it hit the underside of the crossbar and into the goal.

The United States could have won the game seven minutes later when it was awarded a penalty kick after Fan Yunjie touched the ball with her hand after going in for a sliding tackle. However, Gao saved Lilly's kick by correctly guessing to the left side. Parlow got a shot off the rebound, but once again Gao, who was stretched across the ground, made a point-blank save. The game ended in a tie just like the World Cup final had a year earlier. The draw was a disappointment for Heinrichs and her team. The Chinese, however, celebrated their hard-fought comeback. "I just said to the team afterward, 'They're celebrating and we're disappointed.' And it was a tie. That tells you where we're at," said Foudy.[4]

The United States and China led in the standings with four points, followed by Norway with three. The United States had to defeat Nigeria, which was 0–2, in the final group game to ensure itself passage to the semifinals. That's exactly what would happen. First-half goals from Chastain and Lilly, in addition to a hunderbolt shot by MacMillan in the second half, led the United States to a 3–1 victory on September 20 in Melbourne. At the same time, Norway, which needed a win to advance, defeated China 2–1. China finished third and was eliminated. "We would have loved to have another shot at China. We've got Brazil next, which is a very talented team, so we're only focused on the semifinal," said Foudy.[5]

While the United States prepared to play Brazil in Canberra, Germany faced off against Norway in Sydney. Heinrichs, who never missed the chance to publicly applaud her players, argued that reaching the semis was an accomplishment in itself. "If you look at the eight teams in the Olympics, probably four of the top six teams in the world were in our bracket. So at the end of the day, when you see that we have seven points and that we are advancing and going to Canberra, we are as happy as can be," she said.[6]

Against Nigeria, the Americans went into the match knowing that a win would guarantee advancement, no matter the outcome of the game between China and Norway. But Nigeria did not make the task easy. Like many national teams in the African-playing tradition, the Nigerians displayed raw athleticism, strong ball skills, and fearlessness on every tackle. The Nigerians controlled the ebb and flow of the game, even outshooting the United States 18–10. Despite that, the Americans expertly used their skills and experience to outpace the Nigerians in every part of the field. They would need a similar showing in the semifinals.

Following four days of practice, the United States took on Brazil for a shot at the final. Fearing that Hamm was the one real offensive threat that the Americans had, the Brazilians tried to shut her down. The Brazilian players, known for their free-flowing style, hacked

Hamm to the turf every chance they got. Each time Hamm had the ball, a Brazilian player chopped her down. Time and time again, Hamm tried in vain to get a few touches on the ball before a Brazilian defender swooped down and committed a foul.

With eleven thousand fans looking on at Bruce Stadium in Canberra, the United States and Brazil were deadlocked in a scoreless tie going into the second half. Although the Brazilians' blatant and often-brutal fouling drew three yellow cards, the team did everything in its power to stop Hamm, who responded in the only way that she knew how: She scored.

In a game that produced few scoring chances, Hamm tallied in the sixtieth minute, displaying a combination of skill and opportunism. Chastain took a free kick from the right side from forty-five yards out and bent a drive into the penalty box. Midfielder Lorrie Fair—all five feet, three inches, of her—rose above her defender and looped a header back toward the left post, which is when Brazilian goalkeeper Andreia raced out of her goal but missed the descending ball while lunging for it. She then crashed into Milbrett, who was also charging after the loose ball.

With Milbrett and Andreia lying on the ground, Hamm showed up out of nowhere and tucked the bouncing ball into the net from a steep angle, about a yard from the end line near the left post. "I was just trying to go for the ball. For me, I just wanted to try to create a little bit of havoc in there and I did. I got in [Andreia's] way a bit and Mia was following the play and was able to slot the ball in from a tight angle," said Milbrett.[7] The Brazilians argued that a foul should have been called on Milbrett for taking down Andreia. The referee, Nicole Petignat of Switzerland, did no such thing and the goal stood.

Brazil, playing on four days of rest compared to the Americans' three, gave every ounce of energy it had in the last thirty minutes to scratch out a tie, but the U.S. defense would not be beaten, repelling twelve corner kicks during the match and catching the South Americans offside six times. The Americans won and were now in the gold-medal game, where they would take on Norway. The Norwegians, who recorded a 1–0 win over Germany in the other semifinal, were out for revenge against the United States. The rivalry between the two best women's soccer teams was about to heat up once again.

On September 28, the United States and Norway squared off in Sydney. The gold medal was on the line. The game was a seesaw affair. Five minutes into the match, Chastain ran down a loose ball and touched it left to Foudy, who sent the ball forward to Hamm. She fought off a physical challenge by Norwegian captain Goeril Kringen, then cut the ball into the center of the box, where Milbrett volleyed the ball from eight yards into the top left corner for the 1–0 lead.

The United States continued to apply pressure, but just when it seemed that they would go up 2–0, Norway tied the score in the forty-fourth minute on its only decent chance in the first half. Hege Riise sent a right-side corner kick to Espeseth, who nailed a powerful header into the lower right corner. MacMillan, who was guarding the back post, got a foot on the shot but could not keep it out of the net.

The United States dominated the second half, but it was Norway who made the most of its chances. With eleven minutes left, an error by Mullinix helped Norway. After coming up short on a high cross from Margunn Haugenes, her teammate Ragnhild Gulbrandsen looped a header into the net to put Norway up 2–1.

In the second minute of a three-minute injury time, Milbrett pulled off a miracle. The five-foot, one-inch striker managed to leap over a defender to knock in Hamm's long cross from the right side. The Americans were overjoyed, and sudden-death overtime stood on the horizon.

The deciding play of the match occurred twelve minutes into overtime. Mellgren knocked down Fawcett's attempt to clear a header with her left arm; then she ran onto the ball and scored, to win the gold medal with a 3–2 triumph at Sydney Football Stadium before nearly twenty-three thousand fans.

The goal, although controversial, came after Norway attacked throughout the overtime. The winning play started with Riise, who lofted a long ball to the top center of the penalty area. With Mellgren closing, Fawcett headed it to her left. Mellgren jumped in with a late challenge, swinging her left arm in the path of the ball. It hit just below her elbow, sending it directly into Mellgren's path. Kate Sobrero raised her arm in a desperate search for a hand-ball call, but Mellgren slotted the ball right just under Mullinix's extended left hand. Canadian referee Sonia Denoncourt and her two assistants were unmoved by the protests and the goal stood.

The loss marked just the second time the United States had been defeated in Olympic or World Cup play, with both defeats coming at the hands of Norway, the only team with a winning record against the Americans at 15–13–2. Despite dominating play for most of the game, the Americans surrendered three goals for just the second time in the two Olympic and three World Cup tournaments held to date. "Norway did what they had to do. They kept their game plan very simple and they never gave up," said Heinrichs.[8]

The United States had been knocked off its perch. Heinrichs had come up short despite the Americans' playing a superb tournament. "Maybe we are the best team in the world now," exclaimed Norway coach Per-Matthias Hagmo.[9]

"After that final, our players were in the locker room crying, and at the same time, we could hear Norway next door singing, 'We Are the Champions.' It was like they did the centipede after beating us in the 1995 World Cup," said Foudy.[10]

Once again, the Americans were out for revenge. They got their chance three years later, at the World Cup.

NOTES

1. Conference call, August 9, 2000.
2. News release, U.S. Soccer, August 24, 2000.
3. News conference, September 14, 2000.
4. News conference, September 17, 2000.
5. News conference, September 20, 2000.
6. News conference, September 20, 2000.
7. News conference, September 24, 2000.
8. News conference, September 28, 2000.
9. News conference, September 28, 2000.
10. Brandi Chastain, *It's Not about the Bra* (New York: HarperCollins, 2004), 98.

6

Revenge

The 2003 World Cup was another chance for the United States to demonstrate its superiority. The first World Cup, in 1991, was held in China, and FIFA had once again chosen that country to host the event. In May, the tournament hit a snag. Following the outbreak of the respiratory disease SARS (severe acute respiratory syndrome), which had plagued China and resulted in the death of hundreds of people, FIFA decided to move the tournament to the United States.

Because the United States had successfully hosted the event four years earlier, FIFA officials thought that it was the best country to organize the tournament in the little time that remained before the scheduled start in October. U.S. Soccer and its president Robert Contigugla also thought that having the tournament in the United States would save the WUSA from folding. The league had been suffering from sagging attendance and low television ratings and was quickly running out of money.

"I think that everybody involved, from U.S. Soccer to the players and all of the leadership of the WUSA, desperately wants the league to survive. We all feel that the Women's World Cup will give it its needed injection. Hopefully it will also help identify a couple more investors to buy a couple more teams, and then we would all say that the league's future isn't in doubt. That would really be a wonderful thing," said Heinrichs.[1]

In compensation for losing the World Cup, FIFA allowed China to retain its automatic qualification as host and named the country host for the 2007 edition. FIFA and U.S. Soccer were forced to creatively schedule games. Nine doubleheaders were scheduled in group play—similar to the 1999 format—but organizers had to abandon the practice of simultaneously scheduling the final matches of the group stage owing to conflicts with other events at venues.

U.S. Soccer used six venues to host games. Unlike in 1999, when large stadiums were used, the federation decided on smaller ones. The Home Depot Center in Carson, California, home to the MLS's Los Angeles Galaxy, was chosen ahead of the Rose Bowl in nearby Pasadena. The center opened in June 2003 and was one of the first in a series of soccer-specific stadiums that were sprouting up across MLS. Located on the campus of California State University and nicknamed "the Cathedral of American Soccer," the stadium seated twenty-seven thousand fans and was named to host the final.

MLS's first soccer-specific venue, Columbus Crew Stadium, was also named to host the tournament ahead of Soldier Field, a stadium primarily used for football in the fall. Columbus Crew Stadium opened in 1999 and was the brainchild of Crew owner and tycoon Lamar Hunt. Known primarily as a businessman who bankrolled football teams (founding the American Football League in 1960 and owning the Kansas City Chiefs), Hunt had been involved in soccer since the days of the North American Soccer League. Now the stadium that he had helped build was hosting a Women's World Cup.

The other four venues included Gillette Stadium in Foxboro, Massachusetts; Lincoln Financial Field in Philadelphia; RFK Stadium in Washington, D.C.; and PGE Park in Portland, Oregon. The last venue, which was built in 1926 and renovated in 2001, was an attempt by organizers to spread the tournament across the country to maximize national interest.

"We believe the 2003 World Cup will showcase the greatest women athletes in the world, and it's only right that they have the proper platform for that," said Contigugla.[2]

At the World Cup, sixteen teams, including the United States, were vying for the trophy. The Americans were heavily favored to reach the October 12 final and repeat as champions. China, although no longer going to play before a home crowd, was also a favorite to reach the final. Norway, Germany, Sweden, and Brazil rounded out the field with a shot at the title. "The gap between teams is narrowing all the time. This World Cup should see plenty of surprises," observed China coach Ma Liangxing.[3]

The United States was not hoping for too many surprises, even though it was placed in the so-called "Group of Death"—the name commonly given to the most difficult group at a World Cup. The Americans were drawn into Group A, alongside Sweden, North Korea, and Nigeria. FIFA ranked Sweden fifth and North Korea seventh. Not an easy draw but one the Americans were hopeful they could win once the tournament kicked off on September 20.

Heinrichs was retained as coach but needed to win the tournament to show the federation that she was worthy of keeping her job. Her job was made simple because the roster had many of the players who shined at the 1999 tournament: Scurry, Chastain, Hamm, Foudy, Lilly, MacMillan, Milbrett (photo 6.1), and Fawcett all returned. In the mix, Heinrichs had added some new blood, including striker Abby Wambach, seen by many as Hamm's heir, and midfielder Shannon Boxx, who was named to the World Cup roster without ever playing a game for the national team. For Hamm, Foudy, Lilly, and Fawcett, the tournament marked their fourth World Cup.

The United States had continued to dominate regional opponents after winning the 2002 Women's Gold Cup, which also served as a World Cup qualifying tournament. Even after a 3–0 win over Mexico in the opening game at the Rose Bowl, a tough-talking Heinrichs thought that her players should have won by a bigger margin, especially after her team had outshot Mexico 25–2. "It was not such a satisfying result for us. We felt the game got a little reckless in the second half. While we had chances, we just didn't finish them," she said.[4]

Heinrichs knew that opponents at the World Cup would be a lot tougher. Scoring more goals—even running up the score in some cases—would guarantee a win and scare off future opponents. "We have definitely left open the door for better performances," she said.[5]

The United States would go on to qualify for the World Cup after trouncing Costa Rica 7–0 in the semifinals, then adding the Gold

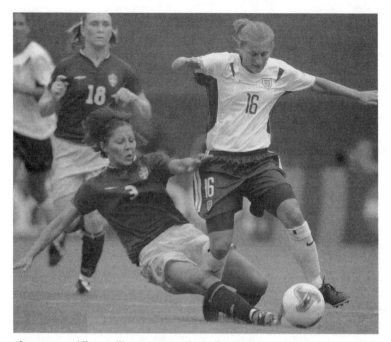

Photo 6.1.   Tiffeny Milbrett powers the ball past the Swedish defense at the 2003 Women's World Cup. (Credit: ISI Photos)

Cup to the team's trophy case with a 2–1 overtime win over Canada. The United States had outscored opponents 24–1 over five games.

If Heinrichs's mind was on scoring goals, then the players' biggest worry was the future of the WUSA. Of the twenty players on the U.S. World Cup roster, only one—UNC defender Cat Reddick—was not playing in the league. Reddick, the youngest player on the team, was a senior and was hoping to play in the league after graduation.

During Labor Day weekend, with just three few weeks before the start of the tournament, Heinrichs convened her players at the Home Depot Center's National Training Center, the new site for the U.S. men's and women's national team players to train ahead of big games and tournaments. The team christened the venue for training camp.

Four days before the start of the World Cup, however, the U.S. players were left stunned. The three-year-old WUSA folded. The league, which rose from the confetti of the 1999 World Cup, was swept away. The announcement's timing could not have been worse. Players were left crestfallen. Morale hit an all-time low. The World Cup became an afterthought. The players were actually banking on the thought that the World Cup would spike interest in the league and spur increased interest from corporate sponsors. That chance would never come. The WUSA was kicked to the curb and was now part of the alphabet soup of acronyms that had made up American soccer history for the better part of a century.

League officials said that they made the announcement on the eve of the World Cup because they could not afford to remain open another day. "We just couldn't keep the doors open for even another 24 hours without jeopardizing a decent and fair severance package for our employees," said John Hendricks, the league's founder and chair of the WUSA board of governors.[6]

Hamm and her teammates were devastated. "You go through a lot of different emotions. The way we feel about it is, it's ours. It's not something that someone else set up and we just showed up. We were a part of it every single step of the way," said Hamm.[7]

Foudy (see p. 88), the player representative on the league's board, gave her teammates the grim news. "The emotional reaction is you fight back tears. Every time I step in front of the team and talk about it, this pit in my stomach just grows and I get teary or I'm fighting tears. What was so special about this league is what it meant to all of us, we never felt entitled," said Foudy, who could not help but cry each time the subject came up.[8]

Hendricks was confident that the players could put this behind them and shine at the World Cup. "My confidence is that these women are so good with dealing with distractions and managing and compartmentalizing distractions that when the time comes they're going to put it away. And after the World Cup is over, they'll start worrying about their next paycheck, their mortgage, cash-flow problems," he said.[9]

The league had also attracted some of the world's best players, including Charmaine Hooper of Canada, Mercy Akide of Nigeria, and Dagny Mellgren of Norway. The WUSA was well on its way to becoming the world's elite women's soccer league before it was forced to close its doors. The dream of making women's soccer into a viable spectator sport in the United States—like basketball had with the WNBA—was on hold. The World Cup beckoned, and national

JULIE FOUDY

Julie Foudy played for the U.S. team at two World Cups, winning both, and at three Summer Olympics, winning the gold medal in 1996 and 2004. A vocal spokeswoman for the team, Foudy was nicknamed "Loudy Foudy" by her teammates. She was team captain from 1991 to 2004.

A University of Stanford standout during her college days, Foudy, a midfielder, retired after the 2004 Athens Games. She was inducted into the National Soccer Hall of Fame in 2007 alongside former teammate Mia Hamm. Foudy found work as a broadcaster, serving

Photo 6.2.   Julie Foudy (left) always used all her grit and determination to win the ball. (Credit: ISI Photos)

as a studio analyst for ABC/ESPN during the 1998 and 2006 men's World Cups. She also worked for the cable network during the 2008 European Championship and helped anchor ESPN's coverage of the 2007 Women's World Cup and Major League Soccer.

Foudy and her husband, Ian Sawyers, currently run the Julie Foudy Sports Leadership Academy for girls aged twelve to eighteen. Foudy has a daughter, Isabel Ann, and a son, Declan.

Appearances: 271

Goals: 45

pride once again took center stage. WUSA grew from the U.S. success at the previous World Cup. This was once again the chance for Team USA to win a title and put the sport back on the front pages of newspapers and magazines. "I had been intoxicated by what I saw in 1999. I mistakenly believed that level of excitement and support would flow over into a league," said Hendricks.[10]

WUSA's investors handed over $100 million to fund the league—which had eight franchises from New York to San Diego—and some players even took pay cuts to help keep it afloat. After cutting costs, the league was still $16 million in the red.

The United States opened its title defense on September 21 against Sweden at RFK Stadium. The Americans put together an easy victory—steamrolling past the Swedes 3–1 with goals from Lilly, Parlow, and Boxx. Four days later, the United States defeated Nigeria 5–0 at Lincoln Financial Field. The physical match was highlighted by two goals from Hamm and one each from Wambach, Parlow, and Foudy.

Scurry, the hero in net for the United States in 1999, recorded the shutout. She had gained nearly twenty pounds before the 2000 Olympics and lost her spot as a starter. At the Olympic final, Scurry watched quietly from the bench as her teammates lost to Norway. "I felt probably deeper sadness than any of them could ever realize, because I felt that it was my fault that they were wearing silver instead of gold. To this day, I still feel that way. I feel like I owe them something," said Scurry.[11]

Since the Olympics, Scurry developed not only a new weight-lifting regimen based on building power but also a new diet based on less junk food and more vegetables. When the WUSA made its debut in 2001, so did a new Scurry. In 2002, the physical differences—her sculpted muscles, quickness, and newfound leaping abilities—were obvious to Heinrichs, who again made her a starter, in time for the World Cup. "You could do a split screen and say, 'Those are two different players, not only visually but what she does on the field,'" said Heinrichs.[12]

The Americans, sitting atop Group A with a 2–0 record, may have been through to the quarterfinals, but they were not done beating opponents. On September 28, the United States took on North Korea, which at 1–1–0, with a win over Nigeria and loss to Sweden, was no longer in contention for a quarterfinal spot. At a sold-out Columbus Crew Stadium in Ohio, the twenty-three thousand fans showed up to watch Hamm and her teammates. Instead, fans never got to see Hamm—except for sitting on the bench. Heinrichs rested her better players—including Chastain (photo 6.3), Boxx, and Parlow—and showed off how deep a talent pool she had at her disposal. For the first time, the United States played in a World Cup game without Hamm. The decision to sit Hamm for the first time in twenty-one World Cup matches, dating to the inaugural tournament in 1991, gave her an extra day's rest before the game against Norway, the runner-up in Group B and the only team to have an all-time winning record against the Americans. Hundreds of girls wearing Hamm replica jerseys and screaming their lungs off were not too happy, although they did not show it given the enthusiasm generated by those in the stands.

Heinrichs said that she would have been comfortable with any of the twenty players on the roster, and her trust was evident against the North Koreans. She used thirteen players in the 2000 Sydney Olympics but inserted eighteen during group play of the 2003 World Cup. Reddick, the only college player on the team, equaled her professional teammates with her heading ability and powerful clearances, not to mention two goals. She used her thigh to redirect a pass from Foudy in the forty-eighth minute, then headed home a crossing pass from MacMillan in the sixty-sixth.

Nine of the eleven U.S. goals in group play resulted from set pieces—once considered a vulnerability for the team. In the seventeenth minute, after a North Korean defender received a yellow card for tugging at Milbrett, Wambach whacked in a penalty kick to open the scoring. "When you can score three goals without [Hamm], you know you have a lot of depth," said Wambach.[13]

Photo 6.3. Brandi Chastain will always be remembered for her winning goal—and her subsequent shirt-removing celebration—at the 1999 Women's World Cup. (Credit: ISI Photos)

On October 1, the United States and Norway renewed their rivalry at Gillette Stadium. The Americans had hit their stride: The players were healthy, the team was scoring goals, and the defense was on top of its game. More important, the players were hungry to win the title. Before a crowd of twenty-five thousand, the U.S. players were ready.

After nearly two days of watching video of Norway's previous games, Heinrichs tried to get her players angry. Heinrichs showed the players clips of Norway's win over the United States in the 1995 World Cup semifinals. She then reran Norway's overtime win against the United States for the gold medal in the 2000 Olympics—a victory that came after the Americans had beaten the Norwegians during the qualifying round. "I needed to remind them that this was the same team that had ripped their hearts out and had stomped on it. I didn't want to ever forget it," recalled Heinrichs.[14]

Truth was, the players needed no reminder. Hamm, Foudy, and Fawcett played in both those matches. The image of Norwegian players bragging or standing atop the medal stand forever burned in their minds. The players never wanted Norway to beat them again, especially during such a high-stakes game. Lacking the sly give-and-go's and razzle-dazzle of previous games, the Americans fell apart. The sort of passes that shred defenses were lacking, especially from Hamm's feet, but the team did its best to suppress any attempt on the part of Norway to create scoring chances. Mellgren, for instance, who had three goals thus far in the competition, did not get a shot off until late in the second half. The U.S. defense tirelessly clung to Mellgren all evening, and in the end, it paid off. The Americans strung together a methodical and pragmatic game plan in its 1–0 win over Norway on a Wambach goal in the twenty-fourth minute.

"This had been the game I was most concerned about because we had two days rest and they had three. This was a critical night for us. [Norway] brought their A game to the field tonight. That makes us better," said Heinrichs.[15]

The Americans entered the semifinals after outscoring opponents 12–1. They never trailed at the tournament. Awaiting the Americans were the Germans, 7–1 winners over Russia. In the other semifinal, Canada, which stunned China 1–0, would play Sweden. An all–North American final appeared a real likelihood. The Americans were on a roll, and Canada quickly became the tournament's Cinderella team.

On October 5, the United States played Germany for a shot at the final. The Germans had had an easier trip to the semifinals. Germany was grouped with Canada, Argentina, and Japan—not the strongest teams in the world—and was lucky enough to be paired versus Russia, another weak opponent, in the quarters. The story going into the game was whether the United States' airtight defense could halt the German's offensive juggernaut. In the end, offense won by the slimmest of margins. The match put on display the best of women's soccer and provided the twenty-eight thousand fans at PGE Park with a contest between a reigning world champion and a team aspiring to be one.

Down 1–0 at halftime on a goal in the fifteenth minute by Kerstin Garefrekes, Heinrichs's team found itself in an unusual spot. The United States had not trailed in a World Cup match since the

1999 quarterfinals, when Germany led 2–1 before the Americans mounted a win. This time, the situation was different. German goalkeeper Silke Rottenberg was tough to beat all game. Heinrichs's fears came true. A failure to score goals would hurt them. And hurt them it did.

Germany's Birgit Prinz and Maren Meinert, who spent the past few years playing in the WUSA, added goals in stoppage time as the Americans desperately went on the counterattack in an attempt to score. The 3-0 win advanced Germany to the final against Sweden. The United States maintained possession for long stretches but was thwarted at every turn by Rottenberg. "In the first minutes we thought Silke Rottenberg would have a good day, and after the goal I had a feeling things would go well. Both sides played well," said German coach Tina Theune-Meyer.[16]

Germany played the match without defender Steffi Jones, who tore a knee ligament in group qualifying, but Rottenberg resembled a steel curtain, pouncing on every U.S. attempt. The United States had dominated the series 12–3–2 and had not lost to the Germans since 1997. "We are older and more experienced. In 1999, we were a little frightened [against the United States]. This time we knew they were not better than us," said Prinz.[17]

The Americans had to settle for third place following a 3–1 win over Canada at the Home Depot Center on October 11, but the players did not treat it as a consolation prize. In fact, it ushered the beginning of their buildup to the next big goal—the 2004 Olympics in Athens, Greece. "Losses always motivate us. It's something you remember every day in training and it drives you to play better. It will drive us for the next year. There has to be a positive that comes out of it for us," said Foudy.[18]

Germany was crowned World Cup champion on October 12 following a 2–1 overtime victory against Sweden. For the first time, there was an all-European final at a World Cup—another indication that the torch had been passed from the Americans to the Germans. The established elites were overthrown by a new generation of players. The pendulum swung to the old continent, where the established men's game had been the envy of the world. Now Europe could claim that it was home to a women's world champion. As for the Americans, the 2004 Summer Games were a chance to retake what was theirs—and show the world that they could compete in the sport that they helped make popular more than a decade earlier.

NOTES

1. Barry Wilner, "Hamm, Chastain among 20 Named to U.S. World Cup Team," *USA Today*, www.usatoday.com/sports/soccer/national/2003-08-28-wwc-training (accessed August 28, 2003).

2. Andy Gardiner, "USA Exudes Confidence as Repeat Host of Cup," *USA Today*, www.usatoday.com/sports/soccer/world/2003-05-26-wwc-repeat_x.htm (accessed May 26, 2003).

3. Interview, July 17, 2003.

4. Interview, October 27, 2002.

5. Interview, October 27, 2002.

6. Interview, September 16, 2003.

7. Kelly Whiteside, "WUSA's Decision Jolts Players," *USA Today*, www.usatoday.com/sports/soccer/wusa/2003-09-15-wusa-players-reaction (accessed September 16, 2003).

8. Whiteside, "WUSA's Decision Jolts Players."

9. Whiteside, "WUSA's Decision Jolts Players."

10. Interview, September 16, 2003.

11. Vicki Michaelis, "Scurry Back in Shape to Help U.S. Defend Cup," *USA Today*, www.usatoday.com/sports/soccer/national/2003-09-11-scurry-comeback_x.htm (accessed September 11, 2003).

12. Michaelis, "Scurry Back in Shape."

13. Jere Longman, "With Norway Looming, U.S. Shows Off Depth," *New York Times*, www.nytimes.com/2003/09/29/sports/sportsspecial/29soccer.html (accessed September 29, 2003).

14. Interview, September 30, 2003.

15. News conference, October 1, 2003.

16. News conference, October 5, 2003.

17. News conference, October 5, 2003.

18. Interview, October 10, 2003.

7

New World Order

The team entered 2004 with only one goal in mind: Win an Olympic gold medal.

Heinrichs was given another chance as coach, even though the squad failed to win the World Cup the previous year. She was zero for two when it came to success on the international level since she took over for the successful DiCicco in 2000.

The players traveled to Athens without Milbrett, who had gotten into a spat with Heinrichs over playing time and what she called "restriction" on the field.[1] "I wish the team well, but I could no longer play in that environment. Creative players can't be held back. I proved my worth on this team years ago," added Milbrett.[2] Heinrichs would certainly miss the energetic Milbrett. The veteran forward felt stifled by Heinrichs's regimen—on and off the field. Milbrett disliked the way that Heinrichs hastily assembled team dinners, meetings, and videotape sessions. What Milbrett viewed as disorganization, Heinrichs regarded as a new way of motivating and inspiring a team that was still reeling from its third-place finish at the World Cup.

Sure, the team was going to be without one of its most striking personalities and a veteran of the 1999 World Cup victory, but Heinrichs had bigger things on her mind, like making sure the other veterans on the team were up to the task, while searching for young talent yearning for success. The players certainly missed Milbrett. Heinrichs did not. "There are no ill feelings on my part. My goal is to keep this team focused on the task at hand and stay committed to the players that are interested [in playing] for us," said Heinrichs.[3]

Like the 2000 Sydney Games, the soccer portion of the 2004 Olympics was spread out across Greece. Only the medal round was slated to take place in Athens. The issue affecting the team going into the Summer Games was not where they would play but who would be playing. The only thing that appeared certain for Heinrichs as she assembled the team was that veterans such as Hamm, Fawcett, Foudy, Lilly, and Chastain would be playing in their final tournament together.

As the large electronic sign at the national soccer training center in Carson, California counted down the days until the start of the Olympics, a feeling of urgency took over the veterans. "You watch that go and you think: 'I've got two months left in my soccer career. I want to make the best of it,'" said Foudy.[4]

The Athens Games were to serve as the last hurrah for the five players who served as the team's backbone since the start of the program. They were on the last leg of a journey that had turned an obscure woman's sport into an American social phenomenon. "They've paved the road for everybody to follow them. Without Foudy, Hamm (photo 7.1), Lilly, Fawcett, Chastain, it just wouldn't have happened this way," said Heinrichs.[5]

The final mission for these veterans was to avoid being beaten by the very monster they created. Although men's soccer was the world's most popular sport, it was the Americans who popularized the women's game throughout the previous decade. To keep up with the United States, teams around the world pumped more money into their women's national teams. At the start of the new millennium, teams such as Brazil—famous for its dominating men's team—closed the gap. "So many of our followers now believe we should win even when we're sleepwalking," said Heinrichs. "And that's not the case anymore."[6]

While Hamm was at the twilight of her career, her protégé was just at the beginning. Abby Wambach (see p. 98) averaged nearly a goal a game before the start of the Olympics and represented the

Photo 7.1. **Mia Hamm runs circles around New Zealand at the 2004 Athens Olympics. (Credit: ISI Photos)**

new generation of American players. If Hamm played with finesse and style, Wambach was effective using opposite traits. Burly and athletic, she roamed the field like the proverbial bull in a china shop. She barreled down players and intimidated opposing defenders in a way similar to that of professional male players. She had a potent shot and ball movement reminiscent of Brazilian magician Ronaldo.

Wambach was eager to succeed. She was determined to not let down her idols and to help give them one final hurrah. "It's just a burning flame inside of me and inside of everyone else on this team that none of us want to let these older women, these veterans, go out on that note. We want to send them off in the best way, in the way that most of them came in," said Wambach.[7]

Once again, Germany and China were expected to vie with the Americans for the podium, whereas Brazil and Sweden were also powerful. Luckily for the Americans, Norway failed to qualify for the Summer Games. A revival of the great U.S.–Norway matchups of the past was not going to happen this time around. Nonetheless, the Olympic tournament posed some problems for the Americans.

ABBY WAMBACH

Abby Wambach has been a regular on the U.S. team since 2003. She got her start at the University of Florida, where, as a freshman in 1999, she helped the team win the National Collegiate Athletic Association title. In 2002, she was chosen second overall in the Women's United Soccer Association (WUSA) draft by the Washington Freedom. Rather than complete her senior year, Wambach turned pro. Playing alongside Mia Hamm, Wambach mastered her scoring skills and helped the Freedom win the league title. Wambach's impressive showing in the WUSA earned her a spot on the U.S. team, in time for the 2003 Women's World Cup.

Photo 7.2.   Abby Wambach continues to score goals and break records for the United States. (Credit: ISI Photos)

Once the WUSA folded, Wambach trained full-time with the United States and was named to the 2004 Olympic roster. That summer, Wambach lifted the team to victory in the gold-medal match against Brazil when her header gave the United States a 2–1 victory. She finished the year with an impressive thirty-one goals and thirteen assists.

By the end of 2006, Wambach emerged as one of the United States' best all-time scorers. At the end of that year, she had tallied sixty-six goals in eighty-four appearances for the United States. Two goals against New Zealand in 2007 moved her ahead of Cindy Parlow and into fifth place on the all-time list of U.S. scorers. At the 2007 Women's World Cup, Wambach recorded six goals in six games despite getting eleven stitches to her head after a collision with a North Korean player in the first game.

But with success came misfortune. After she was named to the 2008 Olympic roster, Wambach broke her left leg on July 16 against Brazil in the last exhibition before the Olympic tournament. Wambach suffered a fractured tibia and fibula, sidelining her for at least three months and forcing her to miss the Olympics. At the time of the injury, Wambach was the leading scorer among active players, just one short of one hundred goals.

When the Women's Professional Soccer got off the ground in 2009, Wambach was assigned to play for the Freedom once again in the league's allocation draft. On July 19, 2009, Wambach scored her one hundredth goal (in just 129 games) in a U.S. jersey during a 1–0 win over Canada in an exhibition match played in her hometown of Rochester, New York.

Appearances: 188
Goals: 143

Ten teams were split unevenly into three groups, forcing the teams in Group G—which included the Americans—to play an extra game. The Americans were slated to play three games in seven days, then a quarterfinal match against an opponent that had at least five more days off. But what appeared to be an advantage for the other teams turned out to favor the Americans in the long run.

The United States was paired off in a relatively easy group, alongside host Greece, Australia, and Brazil. The only formidable opponent was Brazil, whereas Greece, not known for its women's soccer, was forced to field a team and automatically qualified for the tournament. It was the last time that the Greek women would play at an Olympic women's soccer tournament. Australia, however, had participated at world-class tournaments before but has never been a major obstacle for the Americans.

In fact, the United States cruised to a 3–0 win over Greece on August 11, then downed Brazil 2–0 just three days later. The United States had amassed six points—enough for a quarterfinal berth—before even playing Australia. That had been Heinrichs's goal all along. The Americans were in the driver's seat. All they needed against Australia on August 17 was a tie to win the group. The Americans did just that, earning a 1–1 draw and playing without Wambach after she received a one-game ban following consecutive yellow cards against Greece and Brazil. Winning the group pitted the Americans against Japan, an easy quarterfinal opponent, and allowed them to avoid Sweden or Germany.

On August 20, before a paltry crowd of about a thousand at Kafthanzoglio Stadium in Thessaloniki, the United States took on Japan. Wambach regained her starting role as forward alongside Hamm and Lilly. Although the game was tighter than expected, the Americans grabbed the lead right before halftime on a strike from Lilly. Japan's Emil Yamamoto tied the match three minutes into the second half, but Wambach dashed any chance of an upset when she tallied the winning goal with about 30 minutes left to play.

The United States was through to the semifinals to set up a rematch against Germany, who narrowly defeated Nigeria 2–1. Indeed, the elation of beating Japan was short-lived. Knowing that they had to take on Germany conjured up lots of bad memories for the Americans. Heinrichs knew that she needed to at least get to the gold-medal match to hold on to her job. Only Germany stood in the way, but Heinrichs took on an optimistic tone in the days leading up to the game. "It's so easy to get stuck on the past. None of us can predict the future," she said.[8]

At the Athens Games, Heinrichs kept a keen eye on Germany. She watched firsthand as the Germans annihilated China 8–0. Heinrichs downplayed the result, saying that the Chinese had lost only because it played poor defensively and allowed its opponents to score on counterattacks. "It's true that the Germans look impressive when you consider the overwhelming score. But the game could have easily ended 1–0. When they went behind, the Chinese pushed forward to get an equalizer and were punished on the counterattack," she mused.[9]

Unlike the Chinese, the Americans had an experienced roster. A deep bench gave Heinrichs confidence. As the tension mounted in the final stages of the tournament, Heinrichs mixed and matched her players, even cutting down on Chastain's playing time to accommodate younger players such as Cat Reddick and Kate Markgraf. Wambach showed everyone that the hype surrounding her was justified. She scored three goals in as many games—something that Heinrichs heralded by saying, "She embodies the American approach. She knows what she's good at and works hard on her weaknesses."[10] The truth was, Wambach did not have too many weaknesses. She was a physical player—likely the first in the women's game to use her frame to win balls—with the ability to find space and play balls through to her teammates. When she was not dishing out passes, Wambach made sure that she was open in the box to score a goal.

During the World Cup semifinal, Silke Rottenberg put together a fabulous performance in net. She would need a similar showing against a hungry Wambach. Instead, the world champions were in trouble early on. The Americans strung together pass after pass, hoping to wear down the Germans in their August 23 clash at Pankritio Stadium in Heraklion before five thousand fans. The barrage resulted in a goal after thirty-two minutes. Wambach burst down the left flank, teed up a pass for Lilly, who volleyed a left-footed pass just a few yards past Rottenberg.

The United States maintained its dominance in the second half. The hope was to score another goal and put the game away. Hamm had the chance to score the winner with thirty minutes left to play, but her shot went wide. Four minutes later, she once again could have put the match away, but Rottenberg came up with a heroic save. The U.S defense kept the Germans in check all evening. Despite Germany's lack of offensive inspiration, the world champions conjured up some late magic. With the game two minutes into stoppage time, Isabel Bachor charged into the penalty area and fired a shot at Scurry. The ball trickled in for a shock equalizer. The Americans were dejected. Heinrichs threw her hands up in the air. The game was headed to overtime.

The extra session gave both teams newfound energy. The late German comeback reinvigorated the game. The match was now dominated by end-to-end action. The Germans, inspired by their late heroics, had a chance to take the lead, but Kerstin Stegemann blasted the ball high over Scurry. The Americans, refusing to be outdone, could have capitalized on a rare Rottenberg error, but they failed to when Heather O'Reilly's shot slammed against the crossbar.

The Americans were finally rewarded for their offense nine minutes into the first overtime period. Hamm, who was the focal point of the U.S. attack the entire game, burst down the right flank, then cut back a pass from the end line for O'Reilly. This time the striker would not make a mistake, grabbing the loose ball and rifling in a powerful shot past Rottenberg.

The game was not over. The rules set forth by FIFA at these Olympics was to play out the entire thirty-minute overtime session. As a result, the Germans threw everything they had at the U.S. defense. Attempts to score only encouraged the U.S. counterattack to kick into high gear. O'Reilly missed another chance after going one-on-one with Rottenberg, and Germany could have forced a penalty-kick shootout had Renate Lingor's free kick slid wide of Scurry's goal. The Americans effectively ran down the clock for a 2–1 victory. "It's a joy to be the coach of this team. That might have been the best we ever played," said an elated Heinrichs.[11]

The victory against Germany was the biggest in the Heinrichs era. Now the team had to make good on its goal of winning a gold medal. Anything less would leave a mark on the careers of Hamm and the others. The players put their bodies and spirit into this competition and it showed. Up next for the Americans was the gold-medal clash against Brazil, which defeated Sweden 1–0.

Against Brazil on the night of August 26, Heinrichs played her usual 4–4–2 formation with Hamm controlling the midfield and Wambach the target up front. With Chastain doing work on the flank, the Americans were ensured at least a goal—especially against the creative Brazilians, who put their emphasis more on stringing together pretty plays and juggling the ball and less on playing defense.

Brazil, who lost 2–0 to the Americans in the group stage, wanted revenge. They also wanted to score early. They got close. Three minutes into the match, Rosana ended a run with a curling shot from twenty-five yards that went over the crossbar. Three minutes later, they gave the Americans another scare. The Brazilians moved the ball with a grace and finesse that would have made their male counterparts proud. On one of those counterattacks, Scurry thwarted a shot by Elaine.

The Brazilians meant business, but the United States was not easily intimidated. The Americans responded with possession of their own, with Lilly swerving the ball past the Brazilians in an effort to get it to the towering Wambach. The crowd of ten thousand that showed up at Karaisaki Stadium in the city of Piraeus chanted in favor of the Brazilians but were impressed by the Americans each time Hamm got the ball.

The South Americans got more physical with each passing minute. Frustrated that they were not able to score on the Americans early on forced them into a series of crunching tackles and plenty of elbowing. That did not get to the Americans. Using a combination of teamwork and effortless passing, the United States got on the scoreboard in the thirty-ninth minute thanks to a Lindsay Tarpley goal. The goal unleashed wild celebrations in the stands among the healthy group of Americans who showed up to cheer the team on. Scurry did her part in net to preserve her team's 1–0 lead. Cristiane and Daniela had both tried to penetrate Scurry's goal, but were unable to thanks to the goalkeeper's quick reflexes and steady hands.

The game grew increasingly tense in the second half. Brazil felt the urgency of having to score, and Heinrichs ordered her players to pull back and play defense to preserve the lead. Brazil dominated the second period. The Brazilian attack had scored thirteen times during this tournament—five of those tallies coming from Cristiane. However talented they were, the Brazilians were unable to score. The American defense, led by Chastain, played superbly. With seventeen minutes left in the encounter, Brazil got the goal it was looking for all night. Cristiane outpaced Fawcett and crossed the ball low toward Pretinha. Scurry palmed the ball, unable to grab a hold of it, and Pretinha slotted it home from close range. The attendees celebrated—many of them neutral Greek fans simply happy to attend an Olympic event.

In the seventy-fifth minute, Cristiane, in search of a goal, rocketed a shot from twenty-five yards that sailed over Scurry's goal. Two minutes later, Cristiane tried again, only this time it ended up hitting the base of the left post. That part of the goal would turn out to be

Scurry's best friend in stoppage time. With the Brazilian bench and coach Rene Simoes holding their collective breaths on the sidelines, Pretinha saw her shot hit the same post on another play. The Americans got lucky. The plucky Brazilians all but deserved the win. On the other hand, Hamm was a not a factor throughout regulation, unable to find space to make the kind of runs that produced a world-record 153 goals in 266 games. She never once threatened to score.

The game went into overtime with the tired Americans trying to keep up with the unstoppable Brazilians. However, the Americans had both experience and a little luck on their side (photo 7.3). The United States strung together some passes and, after playing defense for nearly fifty straight minutes, finally found the back of the net. With three minutes left in the first overtime period, Lilly swung in a corner kick that Wambach headed into the top corner of the net.

For Wambach (photo 7.4), it was her fourth goal of the competition and eighteenth in twenty games that year. The passing of the

Photo 7.3.   Julie Foudy (right) played her heart out in the gold-medal game at the 2004 Athens Olympics. (Credit: ISI Photos)

Photo 7.4. Abby Wambach uses her size to beat Brazil in the gold-medal game at the 2004 Athens Olympics. (Credit: ISI Photos)

torch was complete. With Hamm and her teammates taking a final bow, Wambach represented the team's future. The players swarmed around Hamm when Swedish referee Jenny Palmqvist blew the whistle for the final time.

Despite being slower, less organized, and less creative than the Brazilians, the Americans once again finished on top. The world's best women's soccer team was awarded the gold medal. Whether they fully deserved it was another matter. The win helped erase the sting of the Americans' loss to Norway in the gold-medal game in Sydney four years earlier and a third-place finish at the 2003 World Cup. In the 1990s, Hamm and her teammates ruled the sport, but other teams caught up. The victory also offered a measure of vindication for Heinrichs, who took over after the 1999 World Cup triumph and failed to win the top prize in 2000 and 2003.

The team was captained for the last time by Foudy, who played the entire 120 minutes just three days after spraining her right ankle in the semifinal victory over Germany. The United States was playing its sixth game in sixteen days—and its second straight 120-minute overtime game. Even so, the Americans found a way to win (photo 7.5). "There are few times in your life where you get to write the final chapter the way you want to," Hamm noted.[12]

Hamm looked to the sky with tears on her cheeks and triumph in her eyes while standing on the podium with her teammates for the medal ceremony. She then blew a kiss to the crowd once the national anthem came to an end. It was the last time that Hamm would play in a tournament donning the U.S. jersey that she helped make famous.

At the postgame news conference, a giddy Heinrichs was over-joyed. In reality, Brazil should have won the game. In the end, heart won over talent. The best team doesn't always get the title. That is what makes soccer such a popular sport the world over. Even an un-derdog can sometimes come out on top; or, in the case of the United

Photo 7.5.   Kristine Lilly (left), Mia Hamm (middle), and Julie Foudy raise their arms in victory on the podium after receiving their gold medals in 2004. (Credit: ISI Photos)

States, a favorite that is having a bad day can always dig deep into its soul and come up with an improbable win. In sports, that is what often separates great from greatness.

"I feel as if the stars, the moon and sun lined up for us to win this gold medal," Heinrichs said.[13] She was also humble toward the Brazilians: "[They] gave us such a great game tonight."[14] When it came to her batch of retiring veterans, Heinrichs said, "We could talk for three hours about them. It's appropriate that they finish on top."[15]

Brazil's time would come. For now, the United States was once again the team to beat.

NOTES

1. Interview, August 19, 2004.
2. Interview, August 19, 2004.
3. Interview, May 3, 2004.
4. *ESPN.com*, "U.S. Women Look to Regain Glory as Vets Retire," sports. espn.go.com/oly/summer04/soccer/news/story?id=1839551 (accessed July 14, 2004).
5. *ESPN.com*, "U.S. Women."
6. *ESPN.com*, "U.S. Women."
7. *ESPN.com*, "U.S. Women."
8. News conference, August 21, 2004.
9. News conference, August 21, 2004.
10. News conference, August 21, 2004.
11. News conference, August 23, 2004.
12. News conference, August 23, 2004.
13. News conference, August 23, 2004.
14. News conference, August 23, 2004.
15. News conference, August 23, 2004.

8

Going Solo

The Heinrichs era came to an end in 2005 when she decided to resign as coach. Still on good terms with U.S. Soccer, Heinrichs opted to go in a different direction and become a consultant for the federation. "It was certainly gratifying to capture the gold medal at the 2004 Olympics, but it is equally gratifying to know that the future is so bright for the talented young players that are moving up through our system. No one is a national team coach forever and for me personally, this is the right time for me to step away," Heinrichs said.[1]

She was replaced with Greg Ryan, a former journeyman defender in the North American Soccer League who successfully coached several women's college programs. Ryan, who had played for the Minnesota Kicks, Tulsa Roughnecks, New York Cosmos, and Chicago Sting over the course of five seasons, garnered praise for his time coaching at the NCAA level.

In 1991, Ryan was named the women's college coach of the year while at the helm at the University of Wisconsin–Madison. In 1996, he moved to Southern Methodist University, where he compiled an astounding 37–21–5 record as the women's head coach. In 1999, he moved back to Colorado College, where he had worked as an assistant coach in the mid-1980s while still a player. Ryan caught the eyes of those at U.S. Soccer after he coached the college's women's team until 2002, compiling an impressive 40–28–6 record. That same year, he was asked to become an assistant under Heinrichs. He was the natural choice for the job once Heinrichs resigned. "Two years is a long time to prepare, so [the players] are happy to be here," said Ryan when speaking about the team's preparations for the 2007 Women's World Cup.[2]

Indeed, with the Olympics behind them, the team's next goal was preparing for the World Cup. Ryan did the best that he could and with a new generation of players at his disposal—many of whom were waiting in the wings since the veterans led the squad to the gold medal in 2004. One veteran who stayed on, however, was Lilly. At age thirty-six, Lilly was set to appear in a record fifth World Cup for the United States. What's more, she was the only female player in the world to play in that many quadrennial tournaments—tying the men's record held by Mexico's Antonio Carbajal and Germany's Lothar Matthaeus. "I wasn't ready to stop. I didn't feel I was at a point where I felt comfortable saying I wanted to leave the game," said Lilly, who was named team captain.[3]

Despite the lack of a pro league, the United States could still rely on the college ranks and semipro teams to produce and nurture the talent that was so vital for the Americans to build a championship-caliber squad. With other nations, such as Brazil, quickly catching up when it came to talent, the Americans were aware that the 2007 tournament, to be played in China, would not be an easy accomplishment. The retirement of players like Hamm had left a void on and off the field. Even Nike, a team sponsor, launched an ad campaign with the phrase, "The greatest team you've never heard of."

With no Hamm to anchor the offense, Ryan made sure that Wambach was her heir. Her physical presence on the field intimidated opposing defenders, even though she lacked the sublime passing and kicking skills that Hamm brought to the team. The Americans were in a state of transition, and Ryan, a polite and quiet man, knew that. He also knew that making sure the players remained cohesive, much in the same way that DiCicco had done nearly a decade earlier, would be the key to success. Women's soccer—and female team sports as a whole—is more about the unit than its individual parts. Unlike male athletes, women did not generally showboat or compete with their teammates for attention or playing time. The coach ran the show from the bench, and the players largely followed. That logic would be put to the test at the World Cup.

For now, Ryan was content with playing a series of friendlies and exhibition tournaments aimed at getting his players plenty of time on the field. Over the span of nearly three years, Ryan went forty-six games without a loss, putting together a 39–0–7 record entering the World Cup, including a 2–0 win over Mexico to qualify for the finals. Hamm might have been gone, but the wins were still there. The winning streak was due in part to the players and in part to Ryan's ability to improvise under tough situations. "He has created an environment for players to grow, to make decisions on their own," said Wambach.[4]

The Americans were paired in the World Cup draw alongside North Korea, which slowly emerged as an Asian power; Sweden (photo 8.1), which was perennially formidable for more than a decade; and Nigeria, one of the strongest teams from Africa. Not a terrible group. If anything, the U.S. team's record going into the

Photo 8.1.   Kate Markgraf does aerial battle with Sweden's Hanna Ljungberg. (Credit: ISI Photos)

competition made them the odds-on favorites, along with Germany and Brazil.

The United States opened the World Cup on September 11 under an incessant rain in the Chinese city of Chengdu in front of thirty-six thousand fans. In what turned out to be a highly entertaining game, the Americans had to settle for a 2–2 draw against the plucky North Koreans. Neither team could find the back of the net in the first half, but all that changed after the break. A Lilly pass to Wambach opened the scoring in the fiftieth minute. Wambach breezed past the North Korean defense before blasting a shot from ten yards to beat goalkeeper Jon Myong Hui. Ryan's 3–4–3 formation, with an equal balance of great defense and dangerous finishing, appeared to be doing the trick.

North Korea came back strong in its quest to level the score. On one of North Korea's offensive forays, a defender collided with Wambach and cracked her head open. Wambach was carted off the field, where she lay on the sidelines—and was later taken to the dressing rooms—for nine minutes while doctors stitched her large wound. As a result, the Americans were forced to defend with one less player because Ryan had refused to sub out his star player. It was during Wambach's absence that North Korea scored both its goals. Kil Son Hui scored a fluke goal after her shot slipped past Solo's wet gloves and went over the line. "It's a day in the life of a goalkeeper. The conditions were slick and wet out there, but it happens," said Solo.[5]

Moments later, Kim Yong Ae scored on a rebound from eight yards out after the ball had been initially blocked by Shannon Boxx. Wambach came back into the game, and the intense end-to-end battle resumed. The Americans tied the score with thirty minutes left to play with Heather O'Reilly in the box off a brilliant pass from Lilly on the left wing. For O'Reilly, it was her first World Cup goal after netting twelve times for the United States going into the match. "It was a pretty great feeling. Pretty awesome. This is every kid's dream," said O'Reilly.[6]

Ryan, upset with the draw, said after the game that his team deserved more and that Wambach's injury helped the North Koreans. "I had our people call over to the locker room to get Abby back as quickly as we can. We knew we were vulnerable," he said.[7] "I had to hurry up the process and yell at the doctors to get it done quicker," added Wambach.[8] In its next game, three days later against Sweden,

Ryan knew that the team needed the win to get out of the group. "The team is ready. They are going to come out and give it everything they've got," Ryan told reporters a day before the game.[9]

The United States and Sweden squared off on September 14 in Chengdu before nearly thirty-one thousand fans under sunny skies and humid conditions. Again, Wambach was the United States' standout player, using her size against the similarly large and physically adept Swedes to lead the Americans to a 2–0 victory.

Ryan used a 4–3–3 lineup with Wambach paired up with Lilly and Lindsay Tarpley, in place of O'Reilly. Ryan's strategy was simple: Play balls long to Wambach until Sweden's defense made a mistake. The tactical change worked, as had so many previous ones hastily put together at the last minute by Ryan. The United States got on the board following a Wambach penalty kick after thirty-four minutes, which she placed perfectly into the left corner of the net. The penalty shot was earned after a Sweden defender chopped down Lori Chalupny, who was just steps away from putting the ball into the empty net.

At halftime, Ryan tinkered with the lineup once again. In was Boxx for Carli Lloyd in a bid to help shore up the midfield against a Sweden side with every intention of trying to tie the score. But with the Swedish attack never able to penetrate Solo's net, Wambach effectively put the game away in the fifty-eighth minute with her second goal of the day. Once again, Lilly, so effective on the left wing, lofted the ball for Wambach in the box. Wambach brought the perfect volley off her chest and powered a shot past a motionless Hedvig Lindahl. "I'm so proud of my players. We knew that this was potentially an elimination match," said Ryan.[10]

The United States' final group match, against Nigeria, was decisive. A win and the Americans would win their group. "We know Nigeria very well. . . . They are very fast, athletic and talented," Ryan said.[11]

On September 18, the Americans faced off against Nigeria under the rain in Shanghai before just sixty-five hundred fans. Despite Nigeria's talent and athleticism, it was the Americans who came out on top. A Chalupny goal just fifty-three seconds into the match on a sloppy, rain-soaked field gave the United States a 1–0 win. The win clinched a spot in the quarterfinals and allowed the Americans to win the group. Afterward, Ryan heaped praise on his players, saying he was "very proud" of them.[12]

As a result, the Americans were paired against England in the quarterfinals and thus avoided the powerful Germans. On the same side of the U.S. bracket, Brazil faced Australia, whereas Germany played North Korea and Norway faced China. "We know that England is a very strong team. . . . They've come a long, long way," noted Ryan.[13] "It's going to be a great match," predicted Lilly.[14]

In Tianjin, the Americans went into the England game on September 22 knowing that they needed to score early if they wanted to break down their opponents. The longer the English kept the Americans off the scoreboard, the better its chances grew of grinding out a result—or, at the very least, pushing the game to overtime. The Americans, however, did not let that happen.

After a scoreless first half that saw few chances for either side, Ryan's team scored three goals in a span of just thirteen minutes to down England 3–0 before nearly thirty thousand fans. The United States got goals from Wambach in the forty-eighth minute, Boxx in the fifty-seventh, and Lilly three minutes later to cap off the win.

The Americans earned two quick corner kicks to start the second half and on the second scored the go-ahead goal. Lilly drove the ball from the left corner into the box where Wambach freed herself of two English defenders to power in a header from close range. The goal marked her fourth tally of the competition. "The first goal is always critical in a match," said Ryan.[15]

The goal did not stop the United States from trying to score another. A left-footed blast from Boxx near the top of the penalty area found the back of the net past England goalkeeper Rachel Brown. Just three minutes later, the United States sealed the win with Lilly, who beat Brown from close range. At the other end of the field, the defense was at the top of its game after posting its third straight shutout with Solo impeccable in net once again (see p. 114).

Despite reaching the semifinals, Wambach said, "We feel like this team hasn't shown its best, and the only way to show our best is to score goals and win games."[16] In other words, the best was yet to come—or so Wambach thought. What would occur in the semis against Brazil would destroy the team and put a program in disarray, especially one based on more than a decade's worth of hard work and dedication.

The team and Ryan would come undone in Hangzhou. Ryan made the blunder of benching Solo (who until that point was having a stellar tournament) and replacing her with the veteran Scurry. The

HOPE SOLO

Hope Solo has slowly emerged as one of the best goalkeepers to ever don a U.S. jersey, but she did not always guard the pipes. As a teen, Solo was a forward before switching positions in college. During her time at the University of Washington, Solo became the team's all-time leader in shutouts, saves, and goals against average.

Before joining the senior U.S. team in 2000, Solo played for several U.S. junior sides. In a span of just eight years, Solo went from being a benchwarmer to a starter and gold-medal winner. After her college career, Solo was drafted in 2003 by the Philadelphia Charge of the WUSA before embarking on a club career in Europe with Sweden's Kopparsbergs/Goteborg in 2004 and France's Olympique Lyon in 2005.

Photo 8.2.   Hope Solo makes one of her trademark flying saves. (Credit: ISI Photos)

At the same time, Solo was named to the 2004 Olympic team but served as a backup to Briana Scurry. She emerged as the team's starting goalkeeper a year later and went a staggering 1,054 minutes without allowing a goal, a streak that ended when the United States defeated France 4–1 at the Algarve Cup.

At the 2007 World Cup, Solo was the United States' starting goalie, giving up two goals in just four games. As the team headed into the semifinals against Brazil, coach Greg Ryan benched Solo in favor of the veteran Scurry, who had a history of great performances against the South Americans. Scurry, however, had not played a full game in nearly three months, and the Americans lost 4–0, which ended a fifty-one-game undefeated streak.

In a postgame interview, an upset Solo blasted Ryan's decision to bench her and Scurry's poor showing in net. Solo was booted from the team and did not play in the third-place match, which the United States won 4–1 over Norway. Solo was part of the team's post–World Cup tour but did not play in any of the three games.

When Ryan's contract was not renewed at the end of 2007, his replacement, Pia Sundhage, named Solo to the Olympic roster in 2008; Scurry was not included. After reconciling with her teammates, Solo returned to the squad as a starter and had a magnificent tournament. Her spectacular performance in the gold-medal match allowed the United States to defeat Brazil 1–0.

Appearances: 124
Goals: 0

move would later come to haunt Ryan—not so much for Scurry's poor performance but for Solo's comments after the match.

On September 27, before fifty thousand, the Americans endured a terrible first half. Brazil scored in the twentieth minute off a corner kick that was spun to the near post. With no Brazilian players close to getting a touch on it, the ball skidded off the grass as midfielder Leslie Osborne dove in an attempt to clear it. Instead, to Scurry's surprise, she inadvertently headed the ball into her own net.

Brazil scored again seven minutes later on a piece of superb dribbling from Marta, who won the ball from defender Stephanie Lopez on the right flank. Marta dribbled inside and darted free, shooting the ball past two defenders that beat Scurry, who could only get a hand on it. Then the situation went from bad to worse.

In desperate need to try to pull one back, Ryan's side found itself down a player after Boxx was ejected. Boxx received an early yellow card (in the fifteenth minute) for upending a Brazilian player and was shown the red during stoppage time. Brazilian forward Cristiane bumped Boxx from behind, and both players went down. In what really was a harsh decision by referee Nicole Petignat, she whistled the foul and sent Boxx to the locker room for an early shower.

With the 2–0 lead and up a player, Brazil possessed the ball in the second period and created play after play using the counterattack. After midfielder Maycon had two close calls in the fiftieth and fifty-second minutes—shots that both skidded past the post—it seemed that Brazil might get another. And it did, in the fifty-sixth minute, when Renata Costa got free down the left flank and played the ball to Cristiane in the middle of the penalty area. She slotted the ball from point-blank range twelve yards away past Scurry.

With Wambach and Lilly unable to create anything offensively, the Brazilians maintained the pressure. Brazil capped off the win in the eightieth minute when Marta took a pass from Costa in the left side of the box with her back to the goal, played the ball around Tina Ellertson, then cut inside to evade Cat Whitehill before rifling it into the lower left corner. Once again, Scurry got a piece of the ball, but it was too powerful for her to turn away. Marta's second tally of the game gave her a tournament-leading seven (photo 8.3).

"The game didn't go our way, but I'm very proud of all of our young women who put in the last two-to-three years of their commitment, time, and dedication, to come out and give their best tonight. To say that, this game is one game, and it's over now, and we're moving on to prepare for [the third-place game] against Norway," said Ryan.[17]

After the game, an incensed Solo, who spent the game on the bench fuming, came out swinging at Ryan's inept decision to sit her in favor of Scurry. Also after the game, Solo publicly blasted Ryan and derided thirty-six-year-old Scurry's performance, saying, "The fact of the matter is, it's not 2004 anymore"—a reference to the United States' gold medal at the 2004 Athens Games in which Scurry was in goal for every minute of every game.[18]

Photo 8.3. Brazilian players celebrate their 4–0 rout over the United States in the semifinals. (Credit: ISI Photos)

Solo clearly violated one of the biggest unwritten rules in sports: Do not criticize your coach or teammates in public. For a team traditionally known for its camaraderie and teamwork, Solo's outburst before an ESPN camera crew was immediately deemed unacceptable. Lilly, who felt denigrated by the comments, decided that Solo would not play in the third-place match against Norway and could not watch from the stands. "The circumstance that happened, and her going public, has affected the whole group. Having her with us would still be a distraction," said Lilly.[19]

Even though her teammates deemed Solo's reaction a distraction, there was some context for her emotional outburst. Her father, Jeffrey, died of heart failure three months before the tournament at the age of sixty-nine. Solo was so emotionally connected to that event that she even sprinkled her father's ashes in the goal area before every game on a mission to take him with her to a world championship. "The only one who really knew me was my father," she said.[20]

Jeffrey Solo would arrive four hours early to watch his daughter warm up during practice, but he never saw her play for the national team in person. He was looking forward to being at the U.S.–Brazil exhibition game on June 23 at Giants Stadium in East Rutherford, New Jersey. Solo said her father hoped to give her a tour of his native Bronx while she was in New York City. It never happened. Jeffrey died just a week before the game. "He was so excited to go back to his hometown, to see me in my USA jersey, to show me where he grew up. Instead, my mom, my brother and I took the trip to honor him. And we took [his ashes] with us. We took him to Yankee Stadium. My dad was the world's only Yankee and Red Sox fan," Solo recalled.[21]

Exiled from the squad after her outburst, Solo posted a statement on her MySpace page, apologizing for her comments:

I have felt compelled to clear the air regarding many of my post-game comments on Thursday night. I am not proud or happy the way things have come out. Although I stand strong in everything I said the true disheartening moment for me was realizing it could look as though I was taking a direct shot at my own teammate. I would never throw such a low blow. Never. Many of this goes way beyond anyone's understanding and is simply hard to justify. In my eyes there is no justification to put down a teammate. That is not what I was doing. I am confidant in knowing that I would have made a major difference on the field. I have to believe that. I have to believe that I should have been on the field or why am I a professional trying to be the very best? I also have agreed to disagree with our head coach and I stand firm in my beliefs that it was the wrong decision. However, to put down a teammate was never, ever my intent. I only wanted to speak of my own abilities yet also recognize that the past is the past. Things were taken out of context, or analyzed differently from my true meaning of my own words. For that I am sorry. I hope everybody will come to know I have a deep respect for this team and for Bri. For all of whom I disappointed, I am truly sorry. There is a fine line of being a professional and being yourself. I can only do what I feel is right, and then hope that my true meaning is understood. I have an uphill battle now, and I have already suffered many consequences. For those who have been in my corner, your support means more than you'll ever know. I cannot thank you all enough. Truly there are too many to respond back to. I feel very fortunate to have the many different people from all different ages, countries and personalities standing behind me. It is extremely humbling. I only wish I could tell you all individually. For those who despise me, well, I can only hope that in due time you can find the understanding needed to forgive me.[22]

The United States took third place, but that was little consolation for a team that failed to win the title and, even worse, remained in tatters.

NOTES

1. News release, February 15, 2005
2. Steven Goff, "U.S. Team Is Ready for the World," *Washington Post*, September 10, 2007, http://www.washingtonpost.com (accessed September 26, 2007).
3. Steven Goff, "U.S. Women Still Have One Link to the Past," *Washington Post*, September 7, 2007, www.washingtonpost.com (accessed September 26, 2007).
4. Goff, "U.S. Team Is Ready."
5. News conference, September 11, 2007.
6. News release, September 11, 2007.
7. News conference, September 11, 2007.
8. News conference, September 11, 2007.
9. News conference, September 13, 2007.
10. News conference, September 14, 2007.
11. News conference, September 14, 2007.
12. News release, September 18, 2007.
13. News release, September 18, 2007.
14. News release, September 18, 2007.
15. News release, September 22, 2007.
16. News release, September 22, 2007.
17. News release, September 27, 2007.
18. *ESPN News*, September 27, 2007.
19. News conference, September 28, 2007.
20. Sal Ruibal and Jill Lieber Steeg, "Hope Solo's World Cup Quest Was for Her Father," *USA Today*, September 30, 2007.
21. Ruibal and Lieber Steeg, "Hope Solo's World Cup Quest."
22. Statement, October 1, 2007.

9

Top of the World Again

Following the Ryan debacle, U.S. Soccer decided to start over.

After gambling on Ryan, who had relatively little experience when it came to the international game, the federation went with former Swedish star Pia Sundhage. Hard to believe, but not a lot of women were coaching women—even as late as 2008. Women coached only two teams at the 2008 Summer Olympics, and Sundhage had been one of them.

Her sometimes unorthodox, laid-back style was just the beginning—she introduced herself to the players on her first day by singing an on-key a cappella version of Bob Dylan's "The Times They Are A-Changin.'"[1] The song came after Sundhage initially met the players inside the dining hall at the Crowne Plaza Hotel near the Home Depot Center in Carson, California, site of the U.S. team's training center. Just as she was about to address the players for the first time, with her nerves jangling and stomach in knots, Sundhage experienced a dose of stage fright.

Just a few hours earlier, Sundhage was alone, having lunch and trying to come up with something to say to the team. The only thing that she could come up with was *forandring*—the Swedish word meaning "change." Sundhage's song was welcomed with tears from some of the players. "I was slightly embarrassed, slightly uncomfortable. But then I was just thinking how cool it was that she's that confident," recalled striker Aly Wagner.[2] That was exactly what Sundhage wanted her players to feel.

U.S. Soccer president Sunil Gulati handpicked Sundhage, who served as an assistant coach on the Chinese team at the 2007 World Cup. Sundhage took the helm in November 2007, less than two months after the team's catastrophic World Cup and just nine months before the start of the Beijing Games.

The players were not the only ones who had obstacles to overcome. As the first foreign-born coach to ever manage the U.S. team, Sundhage said that she introduced herself to the players with a ballad because of her English: "[It's] not my native tongue. . . . I couldn't find the English words. So I sang."[3] All the players knew at that point was that they hit rock bottom at the World Cup and needed a new leader on the bench to inspire them. Even though they finished third, they were outplayed at the World Cup—especially by the Brazilians—and Ryan's decision to bench Solo, and her subsequent comments, left the squad fractured.

Sundhage was a sporting legend back in her homeland. Her face once appeared on a postage stamp, and her two-year stint as an assistant coach and one as a manager in the old WUSA were proof that she had some familiarity with American players. From the start, Sundhage knew that she had to change the team's playing style. The long-ball attack favored by Ryan was the strategy used by inferior teams trying to get past a world power, and it had been beneath the United States all along. Instead of playing the underdog, Sundhage wanted to instill a style fit for a world soccer power. In essence, she wanted to bring passing back to the team and a larger emphasis on individual style and fundamentals. Whereas Ryan coached the United States like it was a college team on a world tour, Sundhage wanted to manage the squad like a world champion trying to defend its title.

The year began with a 4–0 win over Canada on January 16 at the Four Nations tournament in Guangzhou, China. After winning the title, the team traveled to Portugal in March for a shot at the Algarve Cup. Defeating Italy, China, Norway, and Denmark, the team took the trophy, beating their opponents by an impressive total score of 12–1. The United States was back in business.

In April, Sundhage and her team went to Mexico for Olympic qualifying, where they easily qualified, defeating Mexico and Costa Rica and playing Canada to a draw. In May, the team won their first three matches of the year on American soil (overcoming Australia twice) in preparation for the Peace Queen Cup, slated to be played in Suwon, South Korea. The team won all four of its games to collect its third trophy of the year.

The United States' globetrotting adventure did not end in Asia. The team traveled to Scandinavia, where they thumped Norway 4–0 for their first win on Norwegian soil. The team was able to get goals from four players, and it looked to continue its solid play in Sweden three days later. Thanks to a Carli Lloyd goal, the women left Skelleftea with a 1–0 win.

Despite the magnificent string of victories, Sundhage knew that her task at the Olympics would not be a simple one, particularly without Wambach to score the goals. The team was without four players before the start of the tournament. The team was missing not only Wambach but also injured defender Cat Whitehill (formerly known as Cat Reddick) and midfielder Leslie Osborne. Veteran Kristine Lilly opted to take time off to start a family and was not available. Sundhage also tried to mend the rift that had been created by Solo's outburst the previous year. She did so by brining Solo back into the fold and regularly starting her, in a bid to help her regain confidence.

Sundhage tried to mend the differences that Solo's comments created among her teammates. Sundhage asked the players two questions: "Do you want to win?" and "Do you need goalkeepers to win?"[4] The answer to both questions—of course—was an emphatic *yes!* Just like that, Solo was back on the team. At the same time, Sundhage hoped that Solo's success in net would help her teammates come around. It worked. Solo offered her teammates an apology and the group moved on. "It was the wrong decision, and I think anybody who knows anything about the game knows that," Solo said of her postgame rant.[5]

Once in China, the team focused on the task at hand. "You don't have to motivate these players. They are on top of everything and ready to go," said Sundhage.[6] Without the injured Wambach, Sundhage said that her players had to kick it up a notch because acting like nothing was different "would be foolish" and possibly lead to an early exit.[7] "We will put the emphasis on the team," she added.[8] In the opening game on August 6, however, the United States fell behind early to Norway and lost 2-0. It was Sundhage's first defeat as U.S. coach. "I saw more confidence in the U.S. team after they lost to Norway than I did the previous year at the 2007 World Cup when they were winning all their early games," said DiCicco, who worked as a television commentator for NBC during the Olympics.[9]

The team bounced back in its next game with a 1–0 victory over Japan followed by a 4–0 rout of New Zealand to reach the quarterfinals. "My glass is always half full," Sundhage had said after the loss to Norway.[10] After qualifying for the elimination round, the United States faced Canada on August 15 in a tense match. The United States eventually triumphed 2–1 after Natasha Kai scored in overtime on a diving header.

In the semifinals played three days later, the United States took on Japan in an emotional game. Trailing 1–0, the Americans tied the score in the fortieth minute with Angela Hucles after she poked in a low cross from the right side by Heather O'Reilly. Hucles scored again, beating goalkeeper Miho Fukumoto on a tight angle. In between Hucles's goals, Lori Chalupny and O'Reilly both scored. Hucles, who was a benchwarmer under Ryan and never saw any time at the World Cup the previous year, scored two of her tournament-leading four goals against Japan.

Sundhage, elated to have reached the final for a shot at the highest platform on the medal podium, sang Hucles's praises after the game. "She has been one of the most important players on this team since Abby broke her leg," she said.[11]

Indeed, Hucles, a former University of Virginia star, became the team's biggest scoring threat since Wambach's untimely injury on the eve of the competition when she fractured her leg in an exhibition match against Brazil. A combination of quickness in tight spaces and an ability to outmuscle defenders made opponents fear Hucles, although she did not think so. With Wambach, the focus was always on her. Now, opponents do not know whom to focus on. "We have 18 players who can score," Sundhage boasted.[12]

Sundhage said that Hucles was such an "average" player when she first scouted her in 2003 (as coach of the WUSA's Boston Breakers) that she decided to trade her.[13] Asked how the trade went, Sundhage joked, "I got lucky. The league folded."[14] When Sundhage took over as U.S. coach four years later, she said Hucles had vastly improved. "I thought, 'I can't get rid of her a second time.' I told her, 'Angela, you have all the tools, if you just use them.'"[15]

But Solo had a different view, saying opponents do not know what to make of the U.S. team because there are no real stars. "We don't have that Abby Wambach, that Mia Hamm, the Julie Foudy. People don't really know us. Our team is finding so much energy in that. We have so many people scoring goals. . . . We like that we don't have a big-name player."[16]

Brazil once again awaited the United States in the final. The Brazilians defeated world champion Germany 4–1 in the semifinals, sending the United States a dire warning that it meant business. With the 4–0 loss at the World Cup still fresh on their minds, the Americans remained focused. They knew that they had something against Brazil that they could not offer last time: Solo. "I don't think [the World Cup loss] is a personal thing anymore. I think it's now our team thinking, 'We could have won that [World] Cup.'"[17]

Sundhage hit all the right notes as the team prepared to play Brazil. Players such as Kai and Hucles, who played small supporting roles in the past, were thrust into the forefront—and the players had responded with style and verve. The game was the fourth straight Olympic final that the United States was playing in, and it was a rematch of the 2004 gold-medal game in which the United States won 2–1 in overtime. "We have a lot of work to do. They have the big-name players, but we're confident," Solo said of the Brazilians, referring to their biggest threat, two-time FIFA Player of the Year Marta.[18]

On August 21, the United States and Brazil met in the gold-medal match in Beijing. The game turned out to be a scrappy affair, with Solo thwarting effort after effort. The Brazilians danced the samba around the U.S. defense, but Solo was always there to make the save. Solo came off her line on several occasions when the defenders in front of her failed to clear the ball. Her biggest effort came after seventy-two minutes when she made a point-blank save with her right forearm after Marta unleashed a powerful shot that appeared destined for the back of the net.

At the other end of the field, the U.S. attack tried to penetrate the Brazilian defense, although maintaining ball possession for long stretches of the match did little in the way of creating scoring opportunities. As in the 2004 gold-medal game, Brazil got the better of the United States with a series of heart attack-like near misses, although the Americans hung in there and won.

The same thing that occurred in Athens happened in Beijing. With the game deadlocked 0–0, the United States got the winning goal when Amy Rodriguez (see next page), who failed to score on a breakaway attempt near the end of regulation, got around a

AMY RODRIGUEZ

Like national team players that proceeded her, Amy Rodriguez was a star player in college. She graduated from the University of Southern California as the school's fourth all-time scorer, with thirty-one goals, helping the program win its first-ever National Collegiate Athletic Association title as a junior in 2007.

Nicknamed "A-Rod" by her teammates, Rodriguez played for several U.S. youth teams, joining the U.S. national team in 2005 as the only high school player on the roster. She also appeared in two FIFA tournaments, the 2004 Under-19 Women's World Championship in Thailand and the 2006 Under-20 Women's World Championship in Russia.

Photo 9.1. Amy Rodriguez continues to be a standout for the U.S. team. (Credit: ISI Photos)

In 2008, Rodriguez become a regular in the lineup, starting in four of five games at the 2008 Summer Games and scoring against New Zealand. She also assisted on the game-winning goal in the final against Brazil to win the gold medal.

In 2009, the Boston Breakers chose Rodriguez no. 1 overall in the Women's Professional Soccer draft.

Appearances: 37
Goals: 6

defender and laid a pass off to Lloyd, who blasted the ball past Brazilian goalkeeper Barbara. "I'm kind of in shock right now. Never in my wildest dreams would I have thought that I'd score the goal that would win us the World Cup," said Lloyd.[19]

In guiding the team to the gold medal, Sundhage became the first U.S. coach since Dorrance to win a major title on the first try. It was the determination that Sundhage instilled in her players that won the United States the top spot on the podium.

As the Brazilians looked to penetrate the Americans' defense—and miserably failed time and time again to score—the U.S. players grew more and more confident. After ninety minutes of regulation failed to turn up a winner, the dejected and frustrated Brazilians collapsed to the ground. The Americans, meanwhile, just smiled, slowly strutting over to the bench to get a sip of water and talk with Sundhage. "I wasn't tired one bit," recalled Christie Rampone.[20]

Once overtime got underway, the Brazilians succumbed to the pressure, whereas the Americans, relishing their underdog status, played aggressive soccer. They strung together a few passes until Lloyd scored what turned out to be the winner (photo 9.2).

At the final whistle, the Americans rejoiced (photos 9.3 and 9.4). Once again, they were the best women's soccer team on the planet. "We won the gold medal and no one even knows half our names," Markgraf said half-jokingly.[21]

After the Olympics, the team finished the year with an all-time best record of 33–1–2. For Solo, however, winning a gold medal was *the* defining moment. In a year where she had to reconcile with her teammates, helping the squad win the gold was the ultimate apology. "It's like a storybook ending," she said.[22]

Photo 9.2. Carli Lloyd (no. 11) points upward after netting the winning goal against Brazil in overtime to win the gold medal at the 2008 Beijing Olympics. (Credit: ISI Photos)

Photo 9.3. Hope Solo and her teammates embark on a lap of honor around the stadium after winning the gold medal. (Credit: ISI Photos)

Photo 9.4. Natasha Kai (left) and Heather O'Reilly celebrate the gold medal victory with the U.S. flag. (Credit: ISI Photos)

NOTES

1. Mike Woitalla, "No Ordinary Coach," *Soccer America*, December 2008.

2. Michael Silver, "U.S. Women's Soccer Sings Sundhage's Praises," *Yahoo! Sports*, August 5, 2008.

3. Woitalla, "No Ordinary Coach."

4. Jere Longman, "Solo Thwarts Brazil as U.S. Wins Gold in Overtime," *New York Times*, August 22, 2008, D1.

5. Kevin Manahan, "Solo-ing toward the Goal," *Newark Star-Ledger*, August 19, 2008, 49.

6. Conference call, August 3, 2008.

7. Conference call, August 3, 2008.

8. Conference call, August 3, 2008.

9. Woitalla, "No Ordinary Coach."

10. News conference, August 6, 2008.

11. News conference, August 18, 2008.

12. News conference, August 18, 2008.

13. News conference, August 18, 2008.

14. News conference, August 18, 2008.

15. News conference, August 18, 2008.

16. Manahan, "Solo-ing toward the Goal."

17. Manahan, "Solo-ing toward the Goal."

18. Manahan, "Solo-ing toward the Goal."

19. News conference, August 21, 2008.

20. Dan Steinberg, "Lloyd's Goal Is Golden: U.S. Beats Brazil," *Washington Post*, August 22, 2008, E1.

21. Steinberg, "Lloyd's Goal Is Golden."

22. Steinberg, "Lloyd's Goal Is Golden."

10

Golden Again

After capturing the gold medal in Beijing, the United States continued to dominate the world of women's soccer. The team finished both 2009 and 2010 ranked no. 1 by FIFA and was favored, along with Germany, to capture the World Cup in 2011, even though Kristine Lilly had retired. But for all its domination, the United States hit a bump during World Cup qualifying, losing to Mexico 2–1 in Cancún—without Hope Solo in goal, as she was recovering from shoulder surgery—and forcing the Americans to have to endure a two-game, home-and-home tiebreaker against Italy. The United States, despite experiencing the initial scare of possibly missing the World Cup, defeated Italy 1–0 in the first game in Padova, Italy, and by the identical scoreline in the second in Chicago, Illinois, to win the series 2–0. "[After the loss to Mexico], the locker room was disappointed and sad, but it didn't take long to be like, 'OK, we need to take a different road to the World Cup and look at it in a positive way.' The last thing I said in pregame today was that the glass is half full. It's been a bumpy road, but we need to enjoy it, and it will take us all the way to Germany," said Sundhage.[1]

Following the narrow victory against Italy to qualify for the World Cup, the United States returned to its winning ways. Over the six months leading to the finals, the United States retained its top spot

Photo 10.1.   Kristine Lilly, pictured here celebrating a goal with teammate Mia Hamm, retired in 2010 following a twenty-three-year career with the U.S. team. (Credit: HBO)

in the FIFA rankings and posted nine wins and two losses (to Sweden and England) in eleven games. In its final friendly before flying to Europe for the World Cup, the United States defeated Mexico 1–0 at Red Bull Arena in suburban New Jersey on a stoppage-time goal by Lauren Cheney before a sparse crowd of six thousand. "I think the road to the World Cup has been bumpy. In a perfect world, we should have scored a couple of goals today, but my glass is half full. When you look at the game, it was an excellent game because we played well and we created chances, and it was a player coming off the bench, Lauren Cheney, who made the difference. That tells us how important every single player is on this team," said Sundhage.[2]

At the Women's World Cup, the United States got off to a strong start, defeating mysterious North Korea 2–0 on June 28 in Dresden, Germany. North Korea's isolation made scouting the team in person for the U.S. coaching staff nearly impossible. Therefore, the players relied on DVDs of North Korea's previous games, studying them in the days leading up to the game. What they saw was a team capable of fending off superior opponents. Despite the United States' superiority, North Korea put together a spirited showing, dominating stretches of play in the first half in an effort to score the go-ahead goal. The Americans held it together, fending off those attempts as Sundhage encouraged her players from the sideline to attack. Unfazed, the United States put together a series of slick passes to dominate the midfield and made several offensive forays, albeit unsuccessful, with a Cheney shot after eleven minutes that was easily smothered by goalkeeper Hong Myong Hui. The stubborn North Koreans replied with a chance of their own in the thirty-fifth minute, after Solo was forced into action following a powerful shot from Kim Su Gyong. The first half ended scoreless.

In the second forty-five minutes of play, the Americans started strong, determined to score and put the game away. In the fifty-fourth minute, Ali Krieger dribbled down the left flank and found Abby Wambach, who crossed the ball into the box with her right foot. Cheney, who was perfectly positioned, soared into the air and connected to give the United States the 1–0 lead. Like in the first half, the North Koreans had a response. Five minutes after Cheney's goal, Ri Ye Gyong's distance shot had Solo beaten, but the ball hit the top of the crossbar. The game wore on with the Americans using their physical and tactical strength to maintain possession. The United States doubled the score in the seventy-sixth minute, when Rachel Buehler's shot crept inside the post and past Hong's outstretched arm to the delight of the large American crowd in the stands. "It felt great to play the first forty-five minutes and then make a few changes and perform even better in the second half. I am really pleased with the way we scored our goals and how we defended. It was a great start to the World Cup," said Sundhage.[3]

It was a great start for the United States. With North Korea over and done with (the team was ultimately fined $400,000 and banned from participation at the 2015 Women's World Cup after five players failed doping tests), the Americans were ready to take on Colombia four days later in Sinsheim, Germany. The Colombians had come off a 1–0 loss to Sweden and needed a win if they wanted to remain in contention for a berth to the knockout stage. Predictably, the United States cruised to victory over Colombia, posting a 3–0 result that qualified the team to the quarterfinals. Sweden, having won 1–0 over North Korea, was tied for first place with the United States with one game left in the first round.

Against Colombia, the United States broke the deadlock after twelve minutes when Heather O'Reilly scored a fabulous goal. When Colombia lost possession at the edge of the penalty box, O'Reilly fired a shot into the top corner to put the Americans ahead

1–0. After the goal, O'Reilly and Wambach continued to spearhead the attack, trying unsuccessfully to convert again and put the game away. The Americans did just that five minutes into the second period, as halftime substitute Megan Rapinoe tallied off an assist from Cheney. The goal sent Rapinoe into a frenzy with a celebration near the corner-kick flag. Once there, Rapinoe picked up a field microphone and began singing "Born in the U.S.A." to the delight of her teammates, who had gathered around her. Seven minutes later, Carli Lloyd scored the United States' third goal on a long-range shot. Wambach had another brilliant match, but for the second straight game she had failed to score. She had come close several times, including with a shot that slammed against the post late in the game after beating goalkeeper Sandra Sepulveda in a race for a loose ball. "I've got a squad with real experience, but it also contains some younger players who've put in some great performances and made just the right decisions when called upon. I'm especially happy that we were able to create so many chances for ourselves. And although it just wasn't Abby Wambach's day today, I've no doubt she'll start knocking in a few goals soon," said Sundhage.[4]

On July 6, the United States faced Sweden in Wolfsburg, Germany. Both sides were through to the quarterfinals but were playing for first place in the group in order to avoid Brazil in the next round. History was on the United States' side, with the Americans having won all three of its previous World Cup matches against Sweden. In the end, the Americans lost 2–1, condemning Sundhage's squad to second place and a meeting versus Brazil in the quarterfinals. Sweden got Australia in the quarterfinals and a much easier road to the championship game. For the United States, it was the team's first-ever defeat in eighteen first-round games at a World Cup.

Sweden took a 1–0 lead after sixteen minutes after Lotta Schelin was toppled over by Amy LePeilbet in the box. Lisa Dahlkvist hit the penalty kick to score and narrowly beat Solo, who had tried to make the save by diving to her right. Sweden doubled its lead in the thirty-fifth minute following a bad bounce. Swedish captain Nilla Fischer scored a long-range goal; her shot took a deflection that left a confused Solo rooted to the ground. In the second half, the United States attempted a comeback. Wambach, unlucky in her previous two games, finally scored her first goal of the tournament. In the sixty-seventh minute, Wambach tallied the desperately needed goal, heading the ball into the net off a corner kick. For Wambach, it was her tenth all-time World Cup goal. The Americans spent the final twenty minutes desperately seeking to tie the score, but it never came to be. The United States came close in the eighty-sixth minute, but Kelley O'Hara was unable to score off a shot from fifteen yards out. "It was a very good game, very entertaining, and my team played very well. I am happy that we have created many chances, but I am sad that we have lost the game. We could have been more patient with our play," said Sundhage.[5]

Former U.S. captain Julie Foudy, an ESPN color commentator during the tournament, had warned on the eve of the World Cup that the Americans were in no position to take any opponent for granted. Despite that, Foudy believed that the development of the game in the United States made it so that the Americans were still competitive and able to win another World Cup. "You constantly need to develop. You're seeing all these countries doing great things at the player development level from a young age and we have so many young girls in this country playing, which is a distinct advantage," she said.[6]

On July 10 in Dresden, the United States and Brazil renewed their rivalry in a quarterfinal clash for the ages. The Brazilians featured five-time FIFA World Player of the Year Marta against Wambach. Although the United States had not played Brazil since the 2008 Olympic final in Beijing, the two teams were very familiar with each other—they had faced off twenty-seven times overall and seven times in 2007 and 2008 alone. Eight players from Brazil's roster played in the United States–based pro league Women's Professional Soccer, including Marta. "They have three great attacking players with Marta, Cristiane, and Rosana, but we'll be ready for it. We like to go against the best; we want to beat the best. It feels better to do that and go forward," said Christie Rampone.[7]

Twelve years to the day the United States won the 1999 FIFA Women's World Cup over China in a penalty shootout, the Americans were prepared to make history again. Brazil, of course, was not prepared to roll over. Despite their best efforts, the Brazilians went down early, mistakenly putting the ball into their own goal and giving the United States a 1–0 lead after just seventy-four seconds. Brazil, who had not conceded a goal in the first round, could not withstand the United States' first attacking foray. A Shannon Boxx cross to Wambach was misplayed by the Brazilian defense. The ball was played clumsily by both, and the play ended with Daiane putting the ball inadvertently into her own net.

The Americans, up at halftime, caught a break in the fifty-first minute when Lloyd deliberately played the ball with her hand but was not given a red card by referee Jacqui Melksham of Australia. Lloyd had already been shown a yellow card earlier in the game. The breaks ended there. In the sixty-fifth minute, Rachel Buehler was given a red card for taking down Marta in the box. "When Rachel Buehler was sent off, I think we started to play. It's funny, in the first half we probably got the goal too early because we played too safe and didn't run as much as we could have. We played too direct. When Buehler was sent off, you could see something happened to the team and it was more than a running game and we explored the width. If you look at how we kept possession, Megan Rapinoe came in, and late in the game Tobin Heath as well. Those [players] prepared off the bench and made a difference," said Sundhage.[8]

The Brazilians were awarded a penalty kick, which Cristiane attempted. The kick was saved when Solo correctly dived to her left. Melksham ordered the kick retaken but did not give the U.S. players an explanation as to why. "I was definitely frustrated. I got caught up in the emotions of making that first save. I celebrated. I was excited and by the time I turned back around they were lined up to take another kick," said Solo.[9]

On the do-over attempt, Marta stepped up to the spot and buried the ball into the net with Solo guessing the wrong way. The penalty kick tied the game 1–1 and put the Brazilians in position to finally defeat the United States at a major tournament. With the Americans down a player, Sundhage's team maintained possession, and the game ended tied. "We believe if we do this together, we can beat anybody. Obviously, Brazil has fantastic individual talent and have proven over many years that they are capable of winning games— beating us in fact in big tournaments—so this is not going to be an easy game, but neither will any of the games from here on out," said Wambach.[10]

Overtime beckoned as both sides entered the field reinvigorated. Marta put her stamp on the match once again two minutes into the extra session. In a brilliant individual effort, Marta scored again, putting a left-footed shot into the far post past Solo. The cross appeared to have come from an offside position, but the goal stood. The Brazilians appeared poised to defeat the Americans.

The U.S. players had different thoughts. Wambach and her teammates continued to push forward as the clock came close to winding down. Thirty minutes of overtime were almost over when Brazilian defender Erika was given a yellow card for time wasting, a common occurrence in the men's game but something almost unheard of among women. Melksham correctly added two minutes to the clock, and the Americans were handed another lifeline. Rapinoe, who had entered the game in the second half, sent a long cross from the left side into the box for Wambach. After struggling to score earlier in the tournament, Wambach was able to incredibly connect with the ball, putting it into the net. The improbable goal sent the American players into a frenzied celebration. With the score tied, the game would be decided on a shootout. The persistent Americans, who had been down a player for fifty-five minutes, had mounted an incredible comeback. For Wambach, it was the biggest goal of her career and the latest strike ever scored at a Women's World Cup. It was also one of the greatest sports moments of the year.

In the shootout, the Americans shot first. Boxx had her kick saved, but it was ordered retaken after Andreia had rushed off her line early. On her second try, Boxx put the ball into the upper right corner for the goal. Daiane, whose own goal had put the United States ahead, was not accurate with her shot after Solo dived to her right for the save. "I was very confident. It's a hard way to win. It's a hard way to lose. You want the better team to win and I think the better team did win, but sometimes it doesn't always go that way. You never know what is going to happen, but I was confident. We've been practicing; we've been looking good in practice. Everybody was pretty much stone cold. We were ice. I felt like we put them away well," said Solo.[11]

The United States remained perfect on its next three kicks as Lloyd, Wambach, and Rapinoe all scored. When Ali Krieger scored her shot, rolling the ball inside the left post, the Americans had prevailed 5–3 on penalties to reach the semifinals. It had been a heartfelt and heart-stomping victory. "I have no words. Phenomenal. The goal and then the PKs. Someone is writing this book. There is something about the American attitude to find a way to win. Unbelievable," Sundhage said after the game.[12]

A grinning Sundhage had encapsulated the feelings of her players and the fans, saying, "Right now I'm the happiest person on earth. . . . It's hard to put together all the thoughts I have. I want to talk about how emotional I became. There's something to be said about this team. This American attitude of pulling everything together and bringing out the best performance in each other is contagious. I am very, very proud, and I'm very, very happy to be the coach for the U.S. team."[13]

The players were equally thrilled. "I really don't know what to say. I think that is a perfect example of what this country is about, what the history of this team has always been. We never give up. We literally went to the last second it seems. I mean, Hope. How many penalties has she saved legitimately today? We never gave up. Brazil is a great team. I really don't have many words for this," said Wambach.[14]

The U.S. forward may have garnered most of the attention, but it was Rapinoe who had been the team's midfield engine. Rapinoe was originally a starter on the left wing, but Sundhage had demoted Rapinoe to the bench before the start of the tournament. Rapinoe never let the role of substitute get to her. Instead, she transformed it into a chance to shine and help the team with a series of clutch performances, most notably her assist to Wambach against Brazil. The blond-haired Rapinoe was not necessarily the fastest player on the team, but she was quick with her feet and could create space to get the ball to her teammates. Rapinoe's abilities helped put the United States in the semifinals against France, which had quickly emerged as the tournament's Cinderella team.

On July 13 in Mönchengladbach, Germany, the United States and France met. At stake was a shot at the final. The Americans came into the match on an emotional high following their win over Brazil. The days leading up to the game were loaded with an enthusiasm previously unseen within the U.S. camp. France, meanwhile, had been coming off a great run of its own, reaching the knockout phase and overcoming England 4–3 in a shootout. With increased interest in the United States following the heroics against Brazil, Sundhage's team was prepared to put on another great performance. "After the game against Brazil, there was so much energy. You have to look at that in a positive way because I hope we can use that energy tomorrow. At the same time, we played many minutes," said Sundhage.[15]

Playing under a misty rain, the United States left its mark early, with Cheney scoring the game's first goal in the ninth minute. The speedy Cheney began and ended the play after the French turned over the ball at midfield. Cheney took a settling touch off to Boxx who played the ball left to LePeilbet. The left back got the ball near the sideline to Lloyd, who played a back heel down the wing to

O'Reilly. She then pushed the ball to the end line, crossing a ball that Cheney redirected into the net. The goal looked as if it had come straight out of Barcelona's playbook and was another sign that Sundhage's hard work over the years had helped create an attitude of selfless teamwork among her players.

The goal also awoke the slumbering French. After dominating the midfield for long stretches, the skillful France came close to scoring in the twenty-ninth minute when Louisa Necib played a great ball for Gaetane Thiney. Solo charged toward her in an effort to stop the shot. In a scrappy effort, Thiney tried to chip the ball over Solo, who stuck up her right arm to knock the ball out for a corner kick. Four minutes later, Necib played a pass on a free kick to midfielder Sonia Bompastor, who nearly tied the score. On a free kick on the left wing, Necib dropped a splendid ball for Bompastor, who then hit a left-footed shot from the top of the eighteen-yard box that slammed against the crossbar.

The French didn't give up at the start of the second half. The equalizer was set up in the fifty-fifth minute by French captain Sandrine Soubeyrand, who found Bompastor on the flank. Thiney timed her run perfectly into the center of the box, and Bompastor passed the ball back to her. The cross sailed over Thiney's head and into the goal after Solo was tricked by the slick surface.

With the match tied, Sundhage looked to her bench for some changes. The first saw Alex Morgan come in for Amy Rodriguez in the fifty-sixth minute. Nine minutes later, supersub Rapinoe replaced Lloyd. With Lloyd on the bench, Cheney moved to the center alongside Boxx while Rapinoe took over the left flank, switching from their typical 4–4–2 formation to a 4–5–1. The changes worked. The Americans dominated possession in the midfield, and Rapinoe was once again key in getting the ball forward. "France played very well, but there's something to be said about our players and their heart. There's a reason why these players come off the bench and make a difference because this team is twenty-one players and I'm very proud of them," said Sundhage.[16]

Wambach came close to scoring on two occasions in the first half—she got into the rhythm of the game with Rapinoe there to supply her balls. Rapinoe began the play that resulted in a corner kick, which followed a poor clearance by goalkeeper Bérangère Sapowicz. Cheney whipped the ball in from the right side to the far post, where Wambach buried the ball into the net after a towering

ALEX MORGAN

Alex Morgan is a player who represents the latest generation of American women who have excelled at the game. After graduating from the University of California, Berkeley, as one of the best players in school history, Morgan was drafted no. 1 overall in the 2011 Women's Professional Soccer draft by the Western New York Flash. In doing so, she became the first player in university history ever to be drafted in the first round by a pro soccer team. Morgan and her team went on to win the Women's Professional Soccer title in her rookie season. She recorded four goals over thirteen games in her first pro season.

On the national-team level, Morgan got her first chance to play for the senior squad in March 2010 as a substitute against Mexico. Morgan, a regular on the United States' Under-20 team before making her debut under coach Pia Sundhage, scored her first goal seven months later against China after coming off the bench. She played in eight games for the United States that year, scoring a total of four

Photo 10.2. Alex Morgan became one of the United States' biggest stars in 2011. (Credit: U.S. Soccer)

times. One of the biggest goals of her career came in November 2010, in the first game of a home-and-home playoff series against Italy with a berth to the Women's World Cup on the line. Morgan's tally in Padova gave the United States a 1–0 win and ultimately helped it qualify for the finals.

In 2011, Morgan got more playing time, featuring in eighteen of the team's nineteen games. Although she only started two of those games, Morgan was useful off the bench in the second half. She scored six times that year. At just twenty-two, Morgan was the youngest member of the U.S. team that finished second at the 2011 Women's World Cup. Known for her speed and shooting accuracy, Morgan scored twice during the tournament, which included a goal against France in the semifinals and another versus Japan in the final. She also assisted on Abby Wambach's overtime goal in the final that was eventually lost in a shootout.

Appearances: 26
Goals: 10

header beat the French defense. The goal gave the United States the lead for good. "Megan and other players coming off the bench have made the difference," said Sundhage.[17]

For Wambach, it was her twelfth World Cup strike, tying her for third all-time with Michelle Akers, the U.S. record holder. After the game, a modest Wambach said the victory had been a team effort. "Our team has this ability to stick together when the going gets rough. I couldn't be more excited, more proud. I know we have a lot of friends and family here. I know we have a lot of friends and family back home that are watching and supporting us. We can't do it alone. We know a whole nation is cheering us on. We believe in ourselves, and we are in the final. I couldn't be happier," she said.[18]

The French defense pushed forward in an effort to aid the attack, but the U.S. midfield made sure that any attempt at goal was neutralized. France's attempt was futile and instead allowed the United States to use the counterattack. Morgan used her pace to give the United States the 3–1 win in the eighty-second minute following a brilliant play. LePeilbet slid the ball away from Elodie Thomis, allowing Rampone to play the ball forward, where Wambach was waiting unmarked. Her header found Rapinoe, who played the ball

Photo 10.3. Alex Morgan (center, with arm raised) celebrates with her teammates after scoring a goal during the 2011 Women's World Cup final match between the United States and Japan in Frankfurt, Germany. (Credit: Gallo Images)

forward for Morgan. After letting the ball drift forward, Morgan waited for Sapowicz to go down. Then she flicked a left-footed chip shot that landed in the back of the net. "With big goals like these I kind of black out. I remember [Rapinoe] giving me a great ball down the line, and I think I took one too many touches. But it paid out in the end because I saw the goalkeeper kind of low and thought if I just chip it a little bit I'd get it over her. Finally, I scored my first [World Cup] goal," said Morgan.[19]

Wambach's ability to head balls into the net, Rapinoe's off-the-bench heroics, and Morgan's speed had all gotten the United States to its first World Cup final since 1999. "Obviously there is a lot of courage that goes into heading the ball. I have a unique ability to be able to predict the flight of the ball, and my teammates also have a unique ability of finding me. There's two parts to scoring on set pieces like we do with head goals, and the very first and most important component is having a good service. Lauren Cheney has been doing fantastic for us on corner kicks," said Wambach.[20]

Despite the thrilling performances put together by the United States at the tournament, Sundhage put the victory in perspective, saying, "At times, we didn't play well today, but we found a way to win. Credit to the players' heart and that's what makes it so wonderful to coach for this team."[21]

If the 1999 team with Mia Hamm had been trailblazers that set the standard for female players around the world, then this 2011 U.S. squad was really all about heart and trying to raise that bar. Wambach said, "That's something that's really cool about this team, because you're seeing it in terms of the generation that is the changeover from that 1999 generation and that 1999 World Cup team. Nothing to take away from them because obviously what they did was special. What they did gave us the opportunities that all of us have here, and even players from different countries, by putting women's soccer literally on the world stage and the world map. With the success of the national team in the United States, we believe that we set a standard for other federations to put money into their programs, and you can see that by this semifinal against France. Who knew that France was going to be such a great team? I think some of the 1999 World Cup players probably would say they knew because they were the ones that put in the hard hours."[22]

The United States had reached the final, where it would play Japan for a chance at its first World Cup title since 1999. Japan was a surprise finalist, emerging out of Group A to stun hosts Germany 1–0 in the quarterfinals and Sweden 3–1 in the semifinals. "Japan has obviously gone through a lot in the past few months, and it's been how their country and team have recovered from that. I definitely think that the world feels a lot for Japan and as we do as well," said Buehler.[23]

Despite the praise the American players heaped on the Japanese, the United States had traditionally dominated their opponents. Japan was 0–22–3 against the United States in its previous twenty-five games. However, the final would be different. During its run to the final, the Japanese players admitted that the destruction left behind by an earthquake earlier in the year had given them additional motivation to do well in Germany. Japan coach Norio Sasaki had even showed the players images of the quake-ravaged areas, where the death toll had reached fifteen thousand, ahead of its quarterfinal game against Germany. Before its semifinal match against Sweden,

Sasaki had showed the players images of the rebuilding effort. Before the start of the tournament, the resilient Japan had spent time training in the United States and even played two friendlies versus the Americans in preparation for the World Cup. "Obviously, I knew before coming into the tournament they'd be very good. Luckily we did have our two games with them before the tournament in Columbus [Ohio] and in Cary [North Carolina]. We played them and we beat them both games 2–0 and luckily we had a chance to see how they play to help get us prepared. They are a technical team with very quick and crafty players that move the ball really fast. The speed of play is going to be a bit quicker and they like to play a passing game. I think we're going to have to figure it out and be smart and communicate once again and defend as a collective group. But it will be a great game and we know them pretty well so hopefully we will be successful," said Krieger.[24]

On July 17 in Frankfurt, Germany, before a crowd of forty-nine thousand, the United States and Japan met in the final. After a scoreless first half, the Americans took the lead with Morgan in the sixty-ninth minute after a rocket of a shot found the back of the net. Following a clumsy U.S. defensive effort, Aya Miyama answered ten minutes from the end to force overtime. Wambach scored, as usual, on a header in the 104th minute. With this goal, she tallied her fourth of the tournament and thirteenth in all World Cups, surpassing Akers. The United States appeared to be on its way to winning it all until three minutes from the end, when Japan again equalized on a play that began off a corner kick by Homare Sawa. Sawa's goal was her fifth of the tournament, making her the top scorer. The game was deadlocked at 2–2 after 120 minutes of play. Despite outshooting the Japanese women 27–14 and hitting the woodwork twice (following attempts at goal by Wambach and Rapinoe in the first half), the Americans had been unable to win. The game was headed to penalty kicks. Unlike the 1999 final in which the United States and China played 120 minutes of scoreless soccer before a shootout determined a winner at the Rose Bowl, this championship game had been thrilling, end-to-end affair. It was a fitting end to a wonderful tournament loaded with emotional moments and last-gasp efforts. "I think we have to remember that playing in a final is the highest level and you have to take chances. We weren't sharp enough on the two goals, and that's why we didn't win the game," said Sundhage.[25]

The momentum slipped away from the Americans' grasp once the shootout got underway. After squandering the lead twice, Japan mustered all its energy and poise during the shootout. Goalkeeper Ayumi Kaihori made two clutch saves, and defender Saki Kumagai coolly converted her kick for the 3–1 game winner that sailed past Solo and into the net, lifting Japan to its first world championship. The Japanese players hugged in celebration after the final kick and were showered with confetti as Sawa lifted the trophy. The players then unfurled a banner that read: TO OUR FRIENDS AROUND THE WORLD, THANK YOU FOR YOUR SUPPORT.

For Japan, it was a remarkable turnaround, a victory that pulled at the heartstrings. Japan had been the sentimental favorites going into the tournament and completed the fairytale by winning it all. For the United States, never before had such a string of great performances resulted in no silverware. This time, they were victims of the crapshoot that is a tie-breaking penalty-kick shootout. Despite the loss, the American players became popular back home and did more to reinvigorate interest in women's soccer than anything since the team's World Cup win on home soil in 1999. People had paid attention to their exploits—with some help from ESPN's nonstop coverage of the event—but that served as little consolation to the dejected U.S. team. "I truly believed that this was our tournament to win, and I felt that the entire time. It's heartbreaking, but at the same time I think there was something bigger pulling for Japan. They were the team of the tournament, and if there's any team we're going to lose to, I tip my hat off to them because they have so much class and play with so much passion and they fought and they fought and I really do have so much respect for the team," said Solo.[26]

Indeed, the final may have arguably been the best and most exciting contest between two women's national teams in the history of the game. The tournament—played under the slogan "The Beautiful Side of 20Eleven"—was by far the best-played Women's World Cup since the tournament had been created by FIFA in 1991. Indeed, the tournament set a new benchmark for exciting performances. Twenty-one of the tournament's thirty-two games either ended in a tie, were decided by a shootout, or determined by a single goal—up from fourteen at the 2007 Women's World Cup. At the games themselves, 87 percent of the 900,000 available tickets were sold, for a total of 782,700. TV ratings also surpassed expectations. The final alone on ESPN was seen by an average of 13.5 million Americans—a 7.4

Photo 10.4. Hope Solo, pictured here in a promotional photo for Nike, emerged as one of the players on the U.S. team to secure a series of endorsement deals. (Credit: Nike)

Nielsen rating, more than double for a soccer game on the all-sports cable network. Wambach, Solo, and Morgan became household names. The final was also the sixth most-watched soccer game in U.S. history. Solo was even invited after the tournament to compete on the popular ABC show *Dancing with the Stars*, bringing her into the living rooms of millions of Americans every week and solidifying her place among the country's most popular athletes. Solo, who had already been under contract with Nike, picked up more endorsements after the tournament, signing lucrative deals with Gatorade and Bank of America.

On the field, the bar for the 2015 Women's World Cup in Canada, where the tournament will grow from sixteen to twenty-four teams, has been set even higher. The technical and tactical aspects of the

Photo 10.5. Solo competed on the ABC primetime show *Dancing with the Stars* after her great performances in the net at the Women's World Cup. (Credit: ABC)

women's game have improved by leaps and bounds. For years, the United States had set the standard around the world for women's soccer. Finally, equality and funding made it so that other nations were able to catch up to the Americans. With greater parity came more competition and better games. For the United States, the next World Cup will be yet another chance to test itself against the best and to see if its players can finally claim once again to be the greatest female soccer players on the planet.

In the meantime, the Americans set their sights on being crowned Olympic champions once again. In January 2012, the team dominated the first round of the Confederation of North, Central American and Caribbean Association Football (CONCACAF) Olympic Qualifying Tournament in Vancouver, Canada, outscoring its three opponents 31–0 and reaching the semifinals undefeated. The United States did qualify for the London 2012 Summer Olympics after downing Costa Rica 3–0 at BC Place, an indoor facility with another Olympic connection in that it was used for the 2010 Winter Games. The scoreline may indicate that the game was a rout, but the Americans struggled to dominate after taking the lead in the first half. "You can't take anything for granted. We did score a lot of goals, but Costa Rica, they came out and played well and played hard. Eventually, we got our three goals, but despite that the first goal came quickly, we struggled a little bit. It became an emotional game more so than a tactical one," said Sundhage.[27]

The Americans did one better in the tournament finale on January 29, showing again their consistent form by routing Canada 4–0 before a healthy crowd of 25,000. The attendance was large given that the Americans are rarely a draw outside the United States and that the National Hockey League All-Star Game was played on the same day in Ottawa. Over five games, the United States posted a 5–0 record and outscored all its opponents by a staggering 38–0. The following day, amid the victorious backdrop of having qualified for the London Games, word came that Women's Professional Soccer had suspended the 2012 season, citing an ongoing legal battle with Dan Borislow, a former franchise owner. Four months later, the league announced that it had folded. The lack of a pro league notwithstanding, the U.S. players knew they had a job to do.

The Americans got a favorable draw and were grouped with France, who were semifinalists at the World Cup, and two other relatively weak opponents in Colombia and North Korea. The United States played its opening match on July 25 at Hampden Park in Glasgow, Scotland, defeating France 4–2 but only after coming from two goals behind. France had taken a 2–0 lead after just thirteen minutes. Goals by Wambach and Morgan leveled the match at halftime. In the second half, the Americans took their lead with Lloyd—who had come off the bench for the injured Boxx—in the fifty-fifth minute with a dazzling distance shot. Morgan sealed the win eleven minutes later with her second goal of the game. "It was incredible. We were ice cold. We weren't even fazed going down two goals, and I think that came from the confidence and our preparation. We feel good and we've been training well. It was one of those things where we knew France was good, but we knew we were better. We still had seventy-five minutes left," said Solo.[28]

The Americans clinched a berth to the quarterfinals at Hampden Park, downing Colombia 3–0 in a game highlighted by the physical play on the part of the South Americans. Rapinoe opened the scoring in the thirty-third minute, tallying her first career Olympic goal, to put the United States ahead. Wambach and Lloyd added goals in the second half to put the game away. Aside from coming away with the win, Wambach suffered a black eye after she was hit in the face. "I'm glad that a black eye is the only thing that came out of that game in terms of an injury," said Wambach.[29]

The Americans ended the first round with three wins after edging North Korea 1–0 on July 31 at Old Trafford in Manchester, England, with a goal from Wambach. This effort set them up for a quarter-final clash with New Zealand. By going 3–0–0, the Americans had recorded three wins out of three for the first time ever at an Olympic tournament. Then, however, came the knockout round. A loss meant that the Americans would go home early. New Zealand did not put up much of a challenge when the Americans faced them on August 3 at St. James' Park in Newcastle, England. The Americans won, 2–0, after Wambach had put them ahead after twenty-seven minutes. It marked her fourth tally in as many games. The United States put the game away three minutes from the end when Sydney Leroux scored her first-ever goal at an Olympics. The win put the Americans in the semifinals against Canada on August 6 in Manchester. The game marked the United States' 500th match. After the win over New Zealand, the Americans stood with a record of 388–57–54 in 499 matches. "It's a winning team. They have lived with the pressure. I just look at the team and it feels like they perform under pressure. They like pressure. The harder [the game], the more you get out of them," said Sundhage.[30]

In the semifinals, the United States and Canada put on an epic clash. In what turned out to be another heart-stopping performance, the Americans won 4–3 in overtime after Morgan's goal in the 123rd minute. The goal had helped the United States overcome three deficits in a game highlighted by controversy. When the United States was down 3–2, Canadian goalkeeper Erin McLeod was whistled for wasting time. Referee Christina Pedersen of Norway had verbally warned McLeod at halftime. This time, Pederson had had enough and awarded the Americans an indirect free kick a few yards in the penalty box. Tobin Heath tapped the ball, and Lloyd unleashed a shot that hit a Canadian player's arm. Pedersen immediately whistled a penalty kick. On the ensuing kick with ten minutes left in the game, Wambach calmly slotted the ball past McLeod to make it 3–3.

Although Canadian Christine Sinclair had recorded a hat trick, the never-say-die Americans continued to press forward during overtime. In the end, the Americans were able to complete a come-from-behind performance that was one for the ages. The bitter Canadians lamented the way Pedersen treated them, even complaining that the time-wasting call is something referees rarely whistle. It had been Wambach who at one point caught Pedersen's attention to tell her that Canada was wasting time and that McLeod had been the major culprit. But Sundhage did not want to have anything to do with the controversy. After the match, she highlighted the team's resilience and her player's ability to find ways to win. "The team refuses to lose and always finds a way to win. If you look in their eyes, if you listen to Abby [Wambach], there is something special about this team. I would say it reminds me so much about last year against Brazil. They have an extra gear. I've been lucky to coach them for five years and it is unique," said Sundhage.[31]

By virtue of Japan's victory over France in the other semifinal, the gold-medal game would be a rematch of the previous year's World Cup. The Americans had a score to settle after losing to Japan on penalties, and this time the momentum seemed to be on the side of the United States. "In order to win championships, you've got to play the best teams. Japan is one of the best in the world; they proved that last summer. If they have healthy players and are fit and if we have healthy players and are rested, it's going to be a great game to watch. They're very possession oriented; they're dangerous when their players are on. I think that tonight we showed that we're not willing to give up no matter what," said Wambach.[32]

The Americans made history at London's Wembley Stadium. Before a crowd of eighty thousand—the a record for a women's soccer match at the Olympics—the United States captured its third consecutive gold medal on August 9, downing Japan 2–1 in another thrilling affair. Lloyd, the gold-medal hero at the 2008 Beijing Olympic Games, led the way once again with both goals. Solo had a magnificent game; when the United States was up 2–1 with ten minutes left, Solo came up with a big save. Japan's Mana Iwabuchi nearly equalized when the United States defense lost the ball near the top of the penalty area. Iwabuchi tried to curl a shot toward the back post, but Solo made a diving save from point-blank range to preserve the score and seal the win. "This was a year's worth of work and the sacrifices all of us have had to make for our friends and families, for the players that didn't make the roster, this goes out to all of our fans that cheered us on last summer and were equally as heartbroken as we were," said Wambach. "This year has been trials and tribulations, we lost to Japan a few times, and this win feels like everything has come full circle. I'm so proud of this team for never giving up. It was a team effort for this entire tournament, and it shows what it takes to win championships—it's teamwork and loyalty and trusting in each other."[33]

NOTES

1. News conference, November 27, 2010.
2. News conference, June 5, 2011.
3. News conference, June 28, 2011.
4. News conference, July 2, 2011.
5. News conference, July 6, 2011.
6. Interview, June 23, 2011.
7. News conference, July 10, 2011.
8. News conference, July 10, 2011.
9. News conference, July 10, 2011.
10. News conference, July 10, 2011.
11. News conference, July 10, 2011.
12. News conference, July 10, 2011.
13. News conference, July 10, 2011.
14. News conference, July 10, 2011.
15. News conference, July 13, 2011.
16. News conference, July 13, 2011.
17. News conference, July 13, 2011.
18. News conference, July 13, 2011.
19. News conference, July 13, 2011.
20. News conference, July 13, 2011.
21. News conference, July 13, 2011.
22. News conference, July 13, 2011.
23. News conference, July 14, 2011.
24. News conference, July 14, 2011.
25. News conference, July 17, 2011.
26. News conference, July 17, 2011.
27. News conference, January 27, 2012.
28. News conference, July 25, 2012.
29. News conference, July 28, 2012.
30. News conference, August 3, 2012.
31. News conference, August 6, 2012.
32. News conference, August 6, 2012.
33. News conference, August 9, 2012.

Appendix A

U.S. Women's National Team Year-by-Year All-Time Results, 1985–2012

Date	Opponent	Result	Location
1985			
August 18	Italy	0–1, L	Jesolo, Italy
August 21	Denmark	2–2, T	Jesolo, Italy
August 23	England	1–3, L	Caorle, Italy
August 24	Denmark	0–1, L	Jesolo, Italy
1986			
July 7	Canada	2–0, W	Blaine, Minn.
July 9	Canada	1–2, L	Blaine, Minn.
July 9	Canada	3–0, W	Blaine, Minn.
July 20	China	2–1, W	Jesolo, Italy
July 22	Brazil	2–1, W	Jesolo, Italy
July 25	Japan	3–1, W	Jesolo, Italy
July 26	Italy	0–1, L	Jesolo, Italy
1987			
July 5	Norway	3–0, W	Blaine, Minn.
July 7	Canada	4–2, W	Blaine, Minn.
July 9	Sweden	1–2, L	Blaine, Minn.
July 11	Norway	0–1, L	Blaine, Minn.

Date	Opponent	Result	Location
August 3	China	2–0, W	Tianjin, China
August 13	China	1–1, T	Shenyang, China
December 12	Japan	1–0, W	Taipei, Taiwan
December 15	New Zealand	0–1, L	Taipei, Taiwan
December 16	Australia	6–0, W	Taipei, Taiwan
December 19	Canada	4–0, W	Taipei, Taiwan
December 20	Taiwan	1–2, L	Taipei, Taiwan
1988			
June 1	Japan	5–2, W	Panyu, China
June 3	Sweden	1–1, T	Panyu, China
June 5	Czechoslovakia	0–0, T	Panyu, China
June 8	Norway	0–1, L	Panyu, China
July 22	West Germany	2–1, W	Rimini, Italy
July 24	Italy	1–2, L	Rimini, Italy
July 27	England	0–2, L	Rimini, Italy
July 29	France	1–0, W	Rimini, Italy
1989			
June 21	Poland	0–0, T	Cagliari, Italy
1990			
July 27	Norway	4–0, W	Winnipeg, Canada
July 27	Canada	4–1, W	Winnipeg, Canada
July 29	Norway	4–2, W	Winnipeg, Canada
August 5	USSR	8–0, W	Blaine, Minn.
August 9	England	3–0, W	Blaine, Minn.
August 11	West Germany	3–0, W	Blaine, Minn.
1991			
April 1	Yugoslavia	8–0, W	Varna, Bulgaria
April 2	Bulgaria	3–0, W	Varna, Bulgaria
April 3	Hungary	6–0, W	Varna, Bulgaria
April 5	France	2–0, W	Varna, Bulgaria
April 7	USSR	5–0, W	Varna, Bulgaria
April 18	Mexico	12–0, W	Port-au-Prince, Haiti
April 20	Martinique	12–0, W	Port-au-Prince, Haiti
April 22	Trinidad and Tobago	10–0, W	Port-au-Prince, Haiti
April 25	Haiti	10–0, W	Port-au-Prince, Haiti
April 28	Canada	5–0, W	Port-au-Prince, Haiti

Date	Opponent	Result	Location
May 18	France	4–0, W	Lyon, France
May 25	England	3–1, W	Hirson, France
May 28	Holland	3–4, L	Vianen, Holland
May 30	Germany	4–2, W	Kaiserslautern, Germany
June 5	Denmark	0–1, L	Odense, Denmark
August 4	China	1–2, L	Changchun, China
August 8	China	2–2, T	Yenji, China
August 10	China	3–0, W	Anshan, China
August 30	Norway	0–1, L	New Britain, Conn.
September 1	Norway	1–2, L	Medford, Mass.
October 4	China	1–2, L	Oakford, Pa.
October 12	China	2–0, W	Fairfax, Va.
November 17	Sweden[a]	3–2, W	Panyu, China
November 19	Brazil[a]	5–0, W	Panyu, China
November 21	Japan[a]	3–0, W	Foshan, China
November 24	Taiwan[a]	7–0, W	Foshan, China
November 27	Germany[a]	5–2, W	Guangzhou, China
November 30	Norway[a]	2–1, W	Guangzhou, China
1992			
August 14	Norway	1–3, L	Medford, Mass.
August 16	Norway	2–4, L	New Britain, Conn.
1993			
March 11	Denmark	2–0, W	Agai, Cyprus
March 12	Norway	0–1, L	Agai, Cyprus
March 14	Germany	0–1, L	Agai, Cyprus
April 7	Germany	1–2, L	Oakford, Pa.
April 10	Germany	3–0, W	Atlanta, Ga.
June 12	Canada	7–0, W	Cincinnati, Ohio
June 15	Italy	5–0, W	Mansfield, Ohio
June 19	Italy	1–0, W	Columbus, Ohio
June 21	Canada	3–0, W	Pontiac, Mich.
July 7	Australia	6–0, W	Hamilton, Canada
July 10	Japan	7–0, W	Hamilton, Canada
July 12	Taipei	3–1, W	Hamilton, Canada
July 14	Russia	2–0, W	Hamilton, Canada
July 17	China	1–2, L	Hamilton, Canada
August 4	New Zealand	3–0, W	New Hyde Park, N.Y.

Date	Opponent	Result	Location
August 6	Trinidad and Tobago	9–0, W	New Hyde Park, N.Y.
August 8	Canada	1–0, W	New Hyde Park, N.Y.
1994			
March 16	Portugal	5–0, W	Silves, Portugal
March 18	Sweden	1–0, W	Santa Antonio, Portugal
March 20	Norway	0–1, L	Faro, Portugal
April 10	Trinidad and Tobago	3–1, W	Scarborough, Tobago
April 14	Canada	4–1, W	San Fernando, Trinidad
April 17	Canada	3–0, W	Port of Spain, Trinidad
July 31	Germany	2–1, W	Fairfax, Va.
August 3	China	1–0, W	Piscataway, N.J.
August 7	Norway	4–1, W	Worchester, Mass.
August 13	Mexico	9–0, W	Montreal, Canada
August 17	Trinidad and Tobago	11–1, W	Montreal, Canada
August 19	Jamaica	10–0, W	Montreal, Canada
August 21	Canada	6–0, W	Montreal, Canada
1995			
February 24	Denmark	7–0, W	Orlando, Fla.
March 14	Finland	2–0, W	Faro, Portugal
March 16	Portugal	3–0, W	Portimao, Portugal
March 1	Denmark	0–2, L	Lagos, Portugal
March 19	Denmark	3–3, T	Quaeira, Portugal
	(*Denmark won 4–2 on penalty kicks.*)		
April 11	Italy	3–0, W	Poissy, France
April 12	Canada	5–0, W	St. Maur, France
April 15	France	3–0, W	Strasbourg, France
April 28	Finland	2–0, W	Decatur, Ga.
April 30	Finland	6–0, W	Davidson, N.C.
May 12	Brazil	3–0, W	Tacoma, Wash.
May 14	Brazil	4–1, W	Portland, Ore.
May 19	Canada	9–1, W	Dallas, Tx.
May 22	Canada	2–1, W	Edmonton, Canada
June 6	China[a]	3–3, T	Gavle, Sweden
June 8	Denmark[a]	2–0, W	Gavle, Sweden
June 10	Australia[a]	4–1, W	Helsingborg, Sweden
June 13	Japan[a]	4–0, W	Gavle, Sweden
June 15	Norway[a]	0–1, L	Vasteras, Sweden
June 17	China[a]	2–0, W	Gavle, Sweden
July 30	Chinese Taipei	9–0, W	New Britain, Conn.

Date	Opponent	Result	Location
August 3	Australia	4–2, W	New Brunswick, N.J.
August 6	Norway	2–1, W	Washington, D.C.
1996			
January 14	Russia	8–1, W	Campinas, Brazil
January 16	Brazil	3–2, W	Campinas, Brazil
January 18	Ukraine	6–0, W	Campinas, Brazil
January 20	Brazil	1–1, T	Campinas, Brazil
	(United States won 4–2 on penalty kicks.)		
February 2	Norway	3–2, W	Tampa, Fla.
February 4	Norway	1–2, L	Jacksonville, Fla.
February 10	Denmark	2–1, W	Orlando, Fla.
February 15	Sweden	3–0, W	San Antonio, Tx.
February 17	Sweden	3–0, W	Houston, Tx.
March 14	Germany	6–0, W	Decatur, Ga.
March 16	Germany	2–0, W	Davidson, N.C.
April 20	Holland	6–0, W	Fullerton, Calif.
April 26	France	4–1, W	St. Louis, Mo.
April 28	France	8–2, W	Indianapolis, In.
May 12	Canada	6–0, W	Worcester, Mass.
May 16	Japan	4–0, W	Horsham, Pa.
May 18	China	1–0, W	Washington, D.C.
July 4	Australia	2–1, W	Tampa, Fla.
July 6	Australia	2–1, W	Pensacola, Fla.
July 21	Denmark[b]	3–0, W	Orlando, Fla.
July 23	Sweden[b]	2–1, W	Orlando, Fla.
July 25	China[b]	0–0, T	Miami, Fla.
July 28	Norway[b]	2–1, W	Athens, Ga.
	(United States won in overtime.)		
August 1	China[b]	2–1, W	Athens, Ga.
1997			
February 28	Australia	4–0, W	Melbourne, Australia
March 3	Australia	3–1, W	Bathhurst, Australia
March 5	Australia	3–0, W	Canberra, Australia
April 24	France	4–2, W	Greensboro, N.C.
April 27	France	2–1, W	Tampa, Fla.
May 2	South Korea	7–0, W	Milwaukee, Wis.
May 4	South Korea	6–1, W	St. Charles, Ill.
May 9	England	5–0, W	San Jose, Calif.
May 11	England	6–0, W	Portland, Ore.

Date	Opponent	Result	Location
May 31	Canada	4–0, W	New Britain, Conn.
June 5	Australia	9–1, W	Ambler, Pa.
June 8	Italy	2–0, W	Washington, D.C
October 9	Germany	1–3, L	Duisburg, Germany
October 12	Germany	3–0, W	Salzgitter, Germany
October 30	Sweden	3–1, W	Chattanooga, Tenn.
November 1	Sweden	3–1, W	Chattanooga, Tenn.
November 11	Brazil	2–1, W	Taubate, Brazil
December 13	Brazil	0–1, L	Sao Paulo, Brazil

1998

January 18	Sweden	3–0, W	Guangzhou, China
January 21	China	0–0, T	Guangzhou, China
January 24	Norway	3–0, W	Guangzhou, China
March 15	Finland	2–0, W	Olhao, Portugal
March 17	China	4–1, W	Loule, Portugal
March 19	Norway	1–4, L	Lagos, Portugal
March 21	Sweden	3–1, W	Quarteira, Portugal
April 24	Argentina	8–1, W	Fullerton, Calif.
April 26	Argentina	7–0, W	San Jose, Calif.
May 8	Iceland	6–0, W	Indianapolis, Ind.
May 10	Iceland	1–0, W	Bethlehem, Pa.
May 17	Japan	2–1, W	Tokyo, Japan
May 21	Japan	2–0, W	Kobe, Japan
May 24	Japan	3–0, W	Yokohama, Japan
May 30	New Zealand	5–0, W	Washington, D.C.
June 25	Germany	1–1, T	St. Louis, Mo.
June 28	Germany	4–2, W	Chicago, Ill.
July 25	Denmark	5–0, W	Uniondale, N.Y.
July 27	China	2–0, W	Uniondale, N.Y.
August 2	China	4–0, W	Orlando, Fla.
September 12	Mexico	9–0, W	Foxboro, Mass.
September 18	Russia	4–0, W	Rochester, N.Y.
September 20	Brazil	3–0, W	Richmond, Va.
December 16	Ukraine	2–1, W	Los Angeles, Calif.
December 20	Ukraine	5–0, W	Fresno, Calif.

1999

January 27	Portugal	7–0, W	Orlando, Fla.
January 30	Portugal	6–0, W	Ft. Lauderdale, Fla.

Date	Opponent	Result	Location
February 24	Finland	3–1, W	Orlando, Fla.
February 27	Finland	2–0, W	Tampa, Fla.
March 14	Sweden	1–1, T	Silves, Portugal
March 16	Finland	4–0, W	Quateira, Portugal
March 18	Norway	2–1, W	Albufeira, Portugal
March 20	China	1–2, L	Loule, Portugal
March 28	Mexico	3–0, W	Pasadena, Calif.
April 22	China	2–1, W	Hershey, Pa.
April 25	China	1–2, L	East Rutherford, N.J.
April 29	Japan	9–0, W	Charlotte, N.C.
May 2	Japan	7–0, W	Atlanta, Ga.
May 13	Holland	5–0, W	Milwaukee, Wis.
May 16	Holland	3–0, W	Chicago, Ill.
May 22	Brazil	3–0, W	Orlando, Fla.
June 3	Australia	4–0, W	Portland, Ore.
June 6	Canada	4–2, W	Portland, Ore.
June 19	Denmark[a]	3–0, W	East Rutherford, N.J.
June 24	Nigeria[a]	7–1, W	Chicago, Ill.
June 27	North Korea[a]	3–0, W	Foxboro, Mass.
July 1	Germany[a]	3–2, W	Landover, Md.
July 4	Brazil[a]	2–0, W	Palo Alto, Calif.
July 10	China[a]	0–0, T	Pasadena, Calif.
	(United States won 5–4 on penalty kicks.)		
September 4	Ireland	5–0, W	Foxboro, Mass.
September 26	Brazil	5–0, W	Denver, Colo.
October 3	South Korea	5–0, W	Columbus, Ohio
October 7	Finland	6–0, W	Kansas City, Mo.
October 10	Brazil	4–2, W	Louisville, Ky.
2000			
January 7	Czech Republic	8–1, W	Melbourne, Australia
January 10	Sweden	0–0, T	Melbourne, Australia
January 13	Australia	3–1, W	Adelaide, Australia
February 6	Norway	2–3, L	Ft. Lauderdale, Fla.
February 9	Norway	1–2, L	Ft. Lauderdale, Fla.
March 12	Portugal	7–0, W	Silves, Portugal
March 14	Denmark	2–1, W	Faro, Portugal
March 16	Sweden	1–0, W	Lagos, Portugal
March 18	Norway	1–0, W	Loule, Portugal
April 5	Iceland	8–0, W	Davidson, N.C.

Date	Opponent	Result	Location
April 8	Iceland	0–0, T	Charlotte, N.C.
May 5	Mexico	8–0, W	Portland, Ore.
May 7	Canada	4–0, W	Portland, Ore.
May 31	China	0–1, L	Canberra, Australia
June 2	Canada	9–1, W	Sydney, Australia
June 4	New Zealand	5–0, W	Sydney, Australia
June 8	Japan	4–1, W	Newcastle, Australia
June 11	Australia	1–0, W	Newcastle, Australia
June 23	Trinidad and Tobago	11–0, W	Hershey, Pa.
June 25	Costa Rica	8–0, W	Louisville, Ky.
June 27	Brazil	0–0, T	Foxboro, Mass.
July 1	Canada	4–1, W	Louisville, Ky.
July 3	Brazil	1–0, W	Foxboro, Mass.
July 7	Italy	4–1, W	Central Islip, N.Y.
July 16	Norway	1–0, W	Osnabruck, Germany
July 19	China	1–1, T	Gottigen, Germany
July 22	Germany	1–0, W	Braunschweig, Germany
July 27	Norway	1–1, T	Tromso, Norway
July 30	Norway	1–2, L	Oslo, Norway
August 13	Russia	7–1, W	Annapolis, Md.
August 15	Russia	1–1, T	College Park, Md.
August 20	Canada	1–1, T	Kansas City, Mo.
September 1	Brazil	4–0, W	San Jose, Calif.
September 14	Norway[b]	2–0, W	Melbourne, Australia
September 17	China[b]	1–1, T	Melbourne, Australia
September 20	Nigeria[b]	3–1, W	Melbourne, Australia
September 24	Brazil[b]	1–0, W	Canberra, Australia
September 28	Norway	2–3, L	Sydney, Australia
	(Norway won in overtime.)		
November 11	Canada	1–3, L	Columbus, Ohio
December 10	Mexico	3–2, W	Houston, Tx.
December 17	Japan	1–1, T	Phoenix, Ariz.
2001			
January 11	China	0–1, L	Panyu, China
January 14	China	1–1, T	Hangzhou, China
March 7	Italy	0–1, L	Rieti, Italy
March 11	Canada	0–3, L	Lagos, Portugal
March 13	Portugal	2–0, W	Silves, Portugal
March 15	Sweden	0–2, L	Albufeira, Portugal

Date	Opponent	Result	Location
March 17	Norway	3–4, L	Quarteira, Portugal
June 30	Canada	2–2, T	Toronto, Canada
July 3	Canada	1–0, W	Blaine, Minn.
September 9	Germany	4–1, W	Chicago, Ill.
2002			
January 12	Mexico	7–0, W	Charleston, SC
January 23	Norway	0–1, L	Guangzhou, China
January 25	Germany	0–0, T	Guangzhou, China
January 27	China	2–0, W	Guangzhou, China
March 1	Sweden	1–1, T	Albufeira, Portugal
March 3	England	2–0, W	Ferreiras, Portugal
March 5	Norway	2–3, L	Lagos, Portugal
March 7	Denmark	3–2, W	Montechoro, Portugal
April 27	Finland	3–0, W	San Jose, Calif.
July 21	Norway	4–0, W	Blaine, Minn.
September 8	Scotland	8–2, W	Columbus, Ohio
September 29	Russia	5–1, W	Uniondale, N.Y.
October 2	Australia	4–0, W	Cary, N.C.
October 6	Italy	4–0, W	Cary, N.C.
October 27	Mexico	3–0, W	Pasadena, Calif.
October 29	Trinidad and Tobago	3–0, W	Fullerton, Calif.
November 2	Panama	9–0, W	Seattle, Wash.
November 6	Costa Rica	7–0, W	Seattle, Wash.
November 9	Canada	2–1, W	Pasadena, Calif.
2003			
January 12	Japan	0–0, T	San Diego, Calif.
January 23	Norway	3–1, W	Zhejiang, China
January 26	China	0–2, L	Wuhan, China
January 29	Germany	1–0, W	Shanghai, China
February 16	Iceland	1–0, W	Charleston, S.C.
March 14	Canada	1–1, T	Olhao, Portugal
March 16	Norway	1–0, W	Ferreiras, Portugal
March 18	Sweden	1–1, T	Vila R. San Antonio, Portugal
March 20	China	2–0, W	Vila R. San Antonio, Portugal
April 26	Canada	6–1, W	Washington, D.C.
May 17	England	3–0, W	Birmingham, Ala.

Date	Opponent	Result	Location
June 14	Ireland	5–0, W	Salt Lake City, Utah
July 13	Brazil	1–0, W	New Orleans, La.
September 1	Costa Rica	5–0, W	Los Angeles, Calif.
September 7	Mexico	5–0, W	San Jose, Calif.
September 21	Sweden[a]	3–1, W	Washington, D.C.
September 25	Nigeria[a]	5–0, W	Philadelphia, Pa.
September 28	North Korea[a]	3–0, W	Columbus, Ohio
October 1	Norway[a]	1–0, W	Foxboro, Mass.
October 5	Germany[a]	0–3, L	Portland, Ore.
October 11	Canada[a]	3–1, W	Carson, Calif.
October 22	Italy	2–2, T	Kansas City, Mo.

2004

Date	Opponent	Result	Location
January 12	Mexico	3–1, W	Dallas, Tx.
January 30	Sweden	3–0, W	Zhensen, China
February 1	China	0–0, T	Shenzen, China
February 3	China	2–0, W	Shenzen, China
February 25	Trinidad and Tobago	7–0, W	San Jose, Costa Rica
February 27	Haiti	8–0, W	San Jose, Costa Rica
February 29	Mexico	2–0, W	San Jose, Costa Rica
March 3	Costa Rica	4–0, W	San Jose, Costa Rica
March 5	Mexico	3–2, W	San Jose, Costa Rica
March 14	France	5–1, W	Ferreiras, Portugal
March 16	Denmark	1–0, W	Quarteira, Portugal
March 18	Sweden	1–3, L	Lagos, Portugal
March 20	Norway	4–1, W	Algarve, Portugal
April 24	Brazil	5–1, W	Birmingham, Ala.
May 9	Mexico	3–0, W	Albuquerque, N.M.
June 6	Japan	1–1, T	Louisville, Ky.
July 3	Canada	1–0, W	Nashville, Tenn.
July 21	Australia	3–1, W	Blaine, Minn.
August 1	China	3–1, W	Hartford, Conn.
August 11	Greece[b]	3–1, W	Heraklio, Greece
August 14	Brazil[b]	2–0, W	Thessaloniki, Greece
August 17	Australia[b]	1–1, T	Thessaloniki, Greece
August 20	Japan[b]	2–1, W	Thessaloniki, Greece
August 23	Germany[b]	2–1, W	Heraklio, Greece
August 26	Brazil[b]	2–1, W	Athens, Greece
September 25	Iceland	4–3, W	Rochester, N.Y.
September 29	Iceland	3–0, W	Pittsburgh, Pa.

Date	Opponent	Result	Location
October 3	New Zealand	5–0, W	Portland, Ore.
October 10	New Zealand	6–0, W	Cincinnati, Ohio
October 16	Mexico	1–0, W	Kansas City, Mo.
October 20	Ireland	5–1, W	Chicago, Ill.
October 23	Ireland	5–0, W	Houston, Tx.
November 3	Denmark	1–1, T	East Rutherford, N.J.
November 6	Denmark	1–3, L	Philadelphia, Pa.
December 8	Mexico	5–0, W	Carson, Calif.
2005			
March 9	France	1–0, W	Ferreiras, Portugal
March 11	Finland	3–0, W	Guia, Portugal
March 13	Denmark	4–0, W	Vila R. San Antonio, Portugal
March 15	Germany	1–0, W	Vila R. San Antonio, Portugal
June 26	Canada	2–0, W	Virginia Beach, Va.
July 10	Ukraine	7–0, W	Portland, Ore.
July 24	Iceland	3–0, W	Carson, Calif.
October 16	Australia	0–0, T	Fullerton, Calif.
October 23	Mexico	3–0, W	Charleston, S.C.
2006			
January 18	Norway	3–1, W	Guangzhou, China
January 20	France	0–0, T	Guangzhou, China
January 22	China	2–0, W	Guangzhou, China
March 9	China	0–0, T	Faro, Portugal
March 11	Denmark	5–0, W	Quarteira, Portugal
March 13	France	4–1, W	Faro, Portugal
March 15	Germany	0–0, T	Faro, Portugal
May 7	Japan	3–1, W	Kuamoto, Japan
May 9	Japan	1–0, W	Osaka, Japan
July 15	Sweden	3–2, W	Blaine, Minn.
July 23	Ireland	5–0, W	San Diego, Calif.
July 30	Canada	2–0, W	Cary, N.C.
August 27	China	4–1, W	Bridgeview, Ill.
September 13	Mexico	3–1, W	Rochester, N.Y.
October 1	Chinese Taipei	10–0, W	Carson, Calif.
October 8	Iceland	2–1, W	Richmond, Va.
October 29	Denmark	1–1, T	Gimhae, South Korea

Date	Opponent	Result	Location
October 31	Australia	2–0, W	Cheonan, South Korea
November 2	Netherlands	2–0, W	Suwon, South Korea
November 4	Canada	1–0, W	Seoul, South Korea
November 22	Mexico	2–0, W	Carson, Calif.
November 26	Canada	2–1, W	Carson, Calif.
2007			
January 26	Germany	0–0, T	Guangzhou, China
January 28	England	1–1, T	Guangzhou, China
January 30	China	2–0, W	Guangzhou, China
March 7	China	2–1, W	Silves, Portugal
March 9	Finland	1–0, W	Ferreiras, Portugal
March 12	Sweden	3–2, W	Vila R. San Antonio, Portugal
March 14	Denmark	2–0, W	Vila R. San Antonio, Portugal
April 14	Mexico	5–0, W	Foxboro, Mass.
May 12	Canada	6–2, W	Frisco, Tx.
June 16	China	2–0, W	Cleveland, Ohio
June 23	Brazil	2–0, W	East Rutherford, N.J.
July 14	Norway	1–0, W	Hartford, Conn.
July 28	Japan	4–1, W	San Jose, Calif.
August 12	New Zealand	6–1, W	Chicago, Ill.
August 25	Finland	4–0, W	Carson, Calif.
September 11	North Korea[a]	2–2, T	Chengdu, China
September 14	Sweden[a]	2–0, W	Chengdu, China
September 18	Nigeria[a]	1–0, W	Shanghai, China
September 22	England[a]	3–0, W	Tianjin, China
September 27	Brazil[a]	0–4, L	Hangzhou, China
September 30	Norway[a]	4–0, W	Shanghai, China
October 13	Mexico	5–1, W	St. Louis, Mo.
October 17	Mexico	4–0, W	Portland, Ore.
October 20	Mexico	1–1, T	Albuquerque, N.M.
2008			
January 16	Canada	4–0, W	Guangzhou, China
January 18	Finland	4–1, W	Guangzhou, China
January 20	Finland	1–0, W	Guangzhou, China
March 5	China	4–0, W	Albufeira, Portugal
March 7	Italy	2–0, W	Alvor, Portugal

Date	Opponent	Result	Location
March 10	Norway	4–0, W	Alvor, Portugal
March 12	Denmark	2–1, W	Vila R. San Antonio, Portugal
April 4	Jamaica	6–0, W	Ciudad Juarez, Mexico
April 6	Mexico	3–1, W	Ciudad Juarez, Mexico
April 9	Costa Rica	3–0, W	Ciudad Juarez, Mexico
April 12	Canada	1–1, T	Ciudad Juarez, Mexico
	(United States wins 6–5 on penalty kicks.)		
April 27	Australia	3–2, W	Cary, N.C.
May 3	Australia	5–4, W	Birmingham, Ala.
May 10	Canada	6–0, W	Washington, D.C.
June 15	Australia	2–1, W	Suwon, South Korea
June 15	Brazil	1–0, W	Suwon, South Korea
June 17	Brazil	1–0, W	Suwon, South Korea
June 19	Brazil	2–0, W	Suwon, South Korea
June 21	Canada	1–0, W	Suwon, South Korea
July 2	Norway	4–0, W	Fredrikstad, Norway
July 5	Sweden	1–0, W	Skelleftea, Sweden
July 13	Brazil	1–0, W	Commerce City, Colo.
July 16	Brazil	1–0, W	San Diego, Calif.
August 6	Norway[b]	0–2, L	Qinhuangdao, China
August 9	Japan[b]	1–0, W	Qinhuangdao, China
August 12	New Zealand[b]	4–0, W	Qinhuangdao, China
August 15	Canada[b]	2–1, W	Shanghai, China
	(United States won in overtime.)		
August 18	Japan	4–2, W	Beijing, China
August 21	Brazil	1–0, W	Beijing, China
	(United States won in overtime.)		
September 13	Ireland	2–0, W	Philadelphia, Pa.
September 17	Ireland	1–0, W	East Rutherford, N.J.
September 20	Ireland	2–0, W	Bridgeview, Ill.
November 1	South Korea	3–1, W	Richmond, Va.
November 5	South Korea	0–0, T	Cincinnati, Ohio
November 8	South Korea	1–0, W	Tampa, Fla.
December 13	China	1–0, W	Carson, Calif.
December 17	China	1–0, W	Detroit, Mich.
2009			
March 4	Denmark	2–0, W	Lagos, Portugal
March 6	Iceland	1–0, W	Ferreiras, Portugal

Date	Opponent	Result	Location
March 9	Norway	1–0, W	Ferreiras, Portugal
March 11	Sweden	1–1, T	Faro, Portugal
	(Sweden won 4–3 on penalty kicks.)		
May 25	Canada	4–0, W	Toronto, Canada
July 19	Canada	1–0, W	Rochester, N.Y.
July 22	Canada	1–0, W	Charleston, S.C.
October 29	Germany	1–0, W	Augsburg, Germany
2010			
February 24	Iceland	2–0, W	Vila Real de Santo Antonio, Portugal
February 26	Norway	2–1, W	Olhao, Portugal
March 1	Sweden	2–0, W	Ferreiras, Portugal
March 3	Germany	3–2, W	Faro, Portugal
March 28	Mexico	3–0, W	San Diego, Calif.
March 31	Mexico	1–0, W	Sandy, Utah
May 22	Germany	4–0, W	Cleveland, Ohio
July 13	Sweden	1–1, T	Omaha, Neb.
July 17	Sweden	3–0, W	East Hartford, Conn.
October 2	China	2–1, W	Kennesaw, Ga.
October 6	China	1–0, W	Chester, Pa.
October 28	Haiti	5–0, W	Cancún, Mexico
October 30	Guatemala	9–0, W	Cancún, Mexico
November 1	Costa Rica	4–0, W	Cancún, Mexico
November 5	Mexico	2–1, L	Cancún, Mexico
November 8	Costa Rica	3–0, W	Cancún, Mexico
November 20	Italy	1–0, W	Padova, Italy
November 27	Italy	1–0, W	Bridgeview, Ill.
2011			
January 21	Sweden	2–1, L	Chongqing, China
January 23	Canada	2–1, W	Chongqing, China
January 25	China	2–0, W	Chongqing, China
March 2	Japan	2–1, W	Vila Real de Santo Antonio, Portugal
March 4	Norway	2–0, W	Vila Real de Santo Antonio, Portugal
March 7	Finland	4–0, W	Quarteira, Portugal
March 9	Iceland	4–2, W	Faro, Portugal
April 2	England	2–1, L	London, England
May 14	Japan	2–0, W	Columbus, Ohio

Date	Opponent	Result	Location
May 18	Japan	2–0, W	Cary, N.C.
June 5	Mexico	1–0, W	Harrison, N.J.
June 28	North Korea[a]	2–0, W	Dresden, Germany
July 2	Colombia[a]	3–0, W	Sinsheim, Germany
July 6	Sweden[a]	1–2, L	Wolfsburg, Germany
July 10	Brazil[a]	1–1, T	Dresden, Germany
	(United States won 5–3 on penalty kicks.)		
July 13	France	3–1, W	Mönchengladbach, Germany
July 17	Japan	1–1, T	Frankfurt, Germany
	(Japan won 3–1 on penalty kicks.)		
September 17	Canada	1–1, T	Kansas City, Kan.
September 22	Canada	3–0, W	Portland, Ore.
November 19	Sweden	1–1, T	Glendale, Ariz.
2012			
January 20	Dominican Republic	14–0, W	Vancouver, Canada
January 22	Guatemala	13–0, W	Vancouver, Canada
January 24	Mexico	4–0, W	Vancouver, Canada
January 27	Costa Rica	3–0, W	Vancouver, Canada
January 29	Canada	4–0, W	Vancouver, Canada
February 11	New Zealand	2–0, W	Frisco, Tex.
February 29	Denmark	5–0, W	Lagos, Portugal
March 2	Norway	2–1, W	Lagos, Portugal
March 5	Japan	1–0, L	Faro, Portugal
March 7	Sweden	4–0, W	Parchal, Portugal
April 1	Japan	1–1, T	Sendai, Japan
April 3	Brazil	3–0, W	Chiba, Japan
May 27	China	4–1, W	Chester, Pa.
June 16	Sweden	3–1, W	Halmstad, Sweden
June 18	Japan	4–1, W	Halmstad, Sweden
June 30	Canada	2–1, W	Sandy, Utah
July 25	France[b]	4–2, W	Glasgow, Scotland
July 28	Colombia[b]	3–0, W	Glasgow, Scotland
July 31	North Korea[b]	1–0, W	Manchester, England
August 3	New Zealand[b]	2–0, W	Newcastle, England
August 6	Canada[b]	4–3, W	Manchester, England
	(United States won in overtime.)		
August 9	Japan[b]	2–1, W	London, England

All games for 2012 run through August 9.
[a]Denotes World Cup.
[b]Denotes Summer Olympics.

Appendix B

U.S. Women's National Team All-Time Team Leaders, 1985–2012

Players	Appearances	
1. Kristine Lilly	352	(1987–2010)
2. Mia Hamm	275	(1987–2004)
3. Julie Foudy	272	(1988–2004)
4. Joy Fawcett	239	(1987–2004)
5. Tiffeny Milbrett	204	(1991–2005)

	Scoring	
1. Mia Hamm	158	(in 275 games)
2. Abby Wambach	143	(188)
3. Kristine Lilly	130	(352)
4. Michelle Akers	105	(153)
5. Tiffeny Milbrett	100	(204)

	Assists	
1. Mia Hamm	144	(in 275 games)
2. Kristine Lilly	105	(352)
3. Tiffeny Milbrett	61	(204)
4. Julie Foudy	55	(272)
5. Shannon MacMillan	50	(176)

Players	*Hat Tricks*	
1. Mia Hamm	10	
Abby Wambach	10	
3. Cindy Parlow	8	
4. Michelle Akers	7	
5. Tiffeny Milbrett	4	

Goalkeepers	*Appearances*	
1. Briana Scurry	168	(1994–2007)
2. Hope Solo	124	(2000–2012)
3. Siri Mullinix	45	(1999–2004)
4. Saskia Webber	28	(1992–2000)
5. Mary Harvey	27	(1989–1996)

	Wins	
1. Briana Scurry	130	(in 168 games)
2. Hope Solo	95	(124)
3. Siri Mullinix	24	(45)
4. Mary Harvey	20	(27)
5. Saskia Webber	19	(28)

	Shutouts	
1. Briana Scurry	71	
2. Hope Solo	65	
3. Siri Mullinix	21	
4. Mary Harvey	13	
5. Saskia Webber	13	

All statistics run through August 9, 2012.

Index

Italic page numbers denote photos and/or textboxes.

Aarones, Ann Kristin, 35–36
Akers (Stahl), Michelle, 1–2, 5,
  12–19, 24–25, *26–27*, 28–30, 32,
  34–37, 47–50, 53, 60, 62–66, 72,
  74, 140, 143

Boxx, Shannon, 85, 89–90, 111, 113,
  116, 134, 136, 147

Chalupny, Lori, 112, 123
Chastain, Brandi, 41, 45, 60–65, 67,
  68, 69, 72, 78–81, 85, 90, 96, 101–
  103; 1999 World Cup final, 50
Cheney, Lauren, 131–132, 137, 141

DiCicco, Tony, 23–25, 27–36, 39, 41–
  47, 49, 58–64, 67–69, 72, 95, 123
Dorrance, Anson, 3, 4, *5–7*, 9–10,
  12–20, 23–24; sexual harassment
  scandal, 58–60

Fawcett, Joy, 33, 36, 40, 50, 64, 72,
  75, 78, 81, 85, 92, 96, 103
Fotopoulos, Danielle, 72
Foudy, Julie, 7, 9, 25, 27, 33, 35,
  40, 42, 49, 61–64, 75–79, 82, 85,
  88–89, 90, 92–93, 96, 105, 123,
  134

Gao, Hong, 37, 68, 76–78; 1999
  World Cup final, 50

Hacker, Colleen, 46–47
Hamm, Mia, 7, 9, 12, 15–16, 20,
  24–37, 40–50, 52–53, *54–55*,
  60–65, 67–68, 73, 75–81, 85, 87,
  89–90, 92, 96, 98, 100–101, 104–
  106, 109, 123, 142
Harvey, Mary, 12
Heinrichs, April, 7, *8–9*, 11–12,
  15–16, 18, 25, 31; head coach,

73–79, 84–86, 90, 92–93, 95–96, 100–102, 103, 105–109
Hucles, Angela, 123–124

Jennings, Carin, 11–13, 15, 18

Kai, Natasha, 123–124, *128*
Keller, Debbie, 33, 58–59

Lilly, Kristine, 7, 9, 16, 24, 29–30, 33–35, 37, 40, 42, 53, 58, 61, 63–66, 68, 75–79, *77–78*, 85, 89, 96, 100–101, 103–104, *106*, 109, 112–113, 116–117, 122, 130
Lloyd, Carli, 133, 135, 137, 147–148

MacMillan, Shannon, 42, 49–50, 63, 68, 75–79, 81, 85, 90
Markgraf (Sobrero), Kate, 81, 101, *110*, 126
Medalen, Linda, 17, 48
Milbrett, Tiffeny, 29–30, 34–35, 37, 40–47, 49, 60, 63, 76, 81, 85, *86*, 91, 95
Morgan, Alex, 138, *139–140*, 141, 143, 147
Mullinix, Siri, 44, 74–76, 78, 81

O'Reilly, Heather, 102, 111–112, 123, *128*, 132–133, 138
Overbeck (Werden), Carla, 16, 25, 28, 31, 33, 40, 42, 45, 47, 59, *69*, 74

Parlow, Cindy, 45, 62–63, 78, 89–90

Rampone, Christine, 126, 134, 140
Rapinoe, Megan, 133, 135–137, 140–141, 143, 147

Reddick, Cat. *See* Whitehill (Reddick), Cat
Roberts, Tiffeny, 29–30, 34–35, 37
Rodriguez, Amy, 124, *125–126*, 138
Ryan, Greg, 44, 109–113, 115, 120–121; World Cup controversy, 116
Ryan, Mike, 4–5

Scurry, Brianna, 30, 34–35, 40, 42, *43–44*, 50, 61–68, 75, 85, 89, 101–102, 113; World Cup controversy, 116–117
Solo, Hope, 44, 111–113, *114–115*, 121–124, 126, 132, 135, 138, 144–145, 147–148; World Cup controversy, 116–117
Sundhage, Pia, 115, 120, 123, 126, 130–131, 133, 135–137, 140, 143, 147–148

Tarpley, Lindsay, 103, 112

Venturini, Tisha, 29, 32, 34–35, 37, 40–42, 64

Wagner, Aly, 72, 121
Wambach, Abby, 85, 89, 91–92, 96–97, *98–99*, 100–101, 103–*105*, 109–113, 116, 123, 133, 135–137, 140–141, 143, 145, 148–150
Wen, Sun, 27, 30, 50
Whitehill (Reddick), Cat, 86, 90, 101, 116, 123
Women's Professional Soccer, 99
Women's United Soccer Association, 83, 86, 89, 90, 93; demise, 87; launch, 73

About the Author

Clemente Angelo Lisi is a reporter for the *New York Post* and author of *A History of the World Cup: 1930–2010*. He lives in New York City with his wife, Kate, daughter, Grace, and son, Mark.